THE
INVASION:
EARTH
COMPANION

THE
INVASION:
EARTH
COMPANION

Peter Haining

HEADLINE

Based on the BBC Television Series written by Jed Mercurio.
By arrangement with BBC Worldwide Limited.
Production stills © the British Broadcasting Corporation 1997
except p19 (*Pearson's Magazine*), p39 (Imperial War Museum),
p83 (Corbis-Bettman) and p85 (Hugh Gray).

First published in 1998
by HEADLINE BOOK PUBLISHING

10 9 8 7 6 5 4 3 2 1

ISBN 0 7472 7622 6

Typeset by Letterpart Limited
Reigate, Surrey
Designed by Isobel Gillan
Printed and bound in Great Britain by
Bath Press Colour Books

HEADLINE BOOK PUBLISHING
A division of Hodder Headline PLC
338 Euston Road
London NW1 3BH

INVASION: EARTH – THE VIDEOS

The complete BBC television series is also available on a set of three videos:
VOLUME 1: THE LAST WAR & THE FOURTH DIMENSION
VOLUME 2: ONLY THE DEAD & THE FALL OF MAN
VOLUME 3: THE BATTLE MORE COSTLY & THE SHATTERER OF WORLDS

Available from all good video stockists.
For further information call BMG Video on 0171 384 7500 or write to
INVASION: EARTH/BMG InterAct at PO Box 607, London SW6 4XR

Page 2: Echo astronaut with escape pod at Loch Ness

Pages 4 and 5: nD 'phenomenon' at Kirkhaven

Contents

the WAR
to end
all WARS?

Invasion: *Earth* is the story of the war that *could* end all wars. Twice this century, the world has been engulfed in international conflicts that those who lived and died in believed would be the last battles between mankind. Yet as the Millennium nears, the war that might well bring about the end of life on Earth is more likely to come from space than from the disputes of warring nations on the planet.

Since the end of the Cold War which for years locked the superpowers of America and Russia in an arms race that also saw them conquer space, the most credible scenario for the Third World War is a conflict with an extraterrestrial force. With each passing year, the possibility of humanity being alone in the galaxy is regarded by scientists as increasingly unlikely; while simultaneously, the number of reported sightings of UFOs and alien encounters by members of the public have grown considerably all over the world.

The BBC's six-part serial is, in fact, far more than just the drama-packed story of a threatened alien invasion of the planet. It has an underlying theme of the danger of war and ingeniously combines the final year of the last great conflict – the Second World War of 1939–1945 – with the very near future, perhaps even tomorrow. Just as colonists once cast covetous eyes on other nations, now aliens from worlds far

beyond this galaxy may be planning exactly the same fate for Earth. It is a chilling thought rooted in an inescapable logic. One of the leading characters in the story, Major General David Reece (Fred Ward), the man from the USAF who heads the special NATO task force trying to counter the invasion, comments grimly: 'No nation is prepared for its next war, only for its last.' The inference is clear: all military thinking now is about what is *known* rather than what is not.

The plot jumps from the war-torn London of 1944 when German V-weapons were plunging on to the population to a high-tech RAF military base in the present day, and the group of people at its centre consists of a fascinating mixture of characters. Flight Lieutenant Christopher Drake (Vincent Regan) is the arrogant Tornado fighter pilot who, in shooting down a UFO against specific orders, inadvertently provides the first clues as to what lies ahead. At the same time, other hints in the form of extraterrestrial signals evidently being sent *into* deep space from somewhere on Earth are picked up by computer scientist Nick Shay (Paul J. Medford) and scientific adviser, Dr Amanda Tucker (Maggie O'Neill), both of whom are dedicated researchers into SETI – The Search for Extraterrestrial Intelligence. (See 'The Search for E.T.')

The dramatic crash which opens the story during the Second World War

Early in the story, Tucker and Drake meet accidentally and realising there is a link between their experiences, as well as a mutual attraction, they join forces. When Major General Reece is appointed to investigate the reports, both he and his second-in-command, Squadron Leader Helen Knox (Phyllis Logan) share a sceptical view of the talk of UFOs and favour a more practical foreign-power-at-work solution. But the leading neurosurgeon, Group Captain Susan Preston (Sara Kestelman), and medical officer, Flight Lieutenant Tim Stewart (Bob Barrett), are investigating some unknown tissues and a brain implant. And their discoveries point inescapably to alien interference with human guinea-pigs. When the mysterious figure of the pilot of the crashed UFO is captured by Flight Lieutenant Jim Radcliffe (Jo Dow) and revealed to be Charles Terrell (Anton Lesser), a former Lieutenant in the Royal Engineers who was reported AWOL from a bomb disposal unit *fifty years ago*, the threat of alien invasion begins to become more than idle fancy. All the more so when Terrell reluctantly talks about a peace-loving race of aliens known as the Echoes who have been his friends for half a century, and the evil extraterrestrials known as nDs who threaten them and the people of Earth. The planet, it seems, is caught in the crossfire between these warring aliens – aliens more destructive than anyone could imagine ...

Invasion: Earth is a series with a very nineties feel. It is more concerned with a group of characters and their interaction than in focusing on a central figure. And because of its sf theme, the major task of the cast has been to breathe life into their characters: to make them act, feel and behave like real people in unreal situations. The result is something of a 'gang show' performance (to use a popular film-making term) which developed during the long months of filming. In fact, when the series was in the early days of production, it was still uncertain how a number of the characters were going to stand out, and it was the on-camera performances of certain actors and actresses which helped to finalise this element of the drama. In one particular instance, the role of Squadron Leader Knox played by Phyllis Logan was originally written for a man, Air Commodore Williams, but was substituted on the undoubted strength of Logan's performance. The inclusion of two other female roles in Group Captain Preston and Dr Tucker is also something of a first for a military drama in terms of equal male/female parts.

Invasion: Earth is the BBC's most ambitious project in the field of mainstream science fiction drama since the classic *Quatermass* series of the fifties. A co-production with the American Sci-Fi Channel, each hour-long episode cost just under £1 million, a budget which demonstrates the faith of both organisations in the concept. The result is a triumph of the illusion-maker's art with authentic locations matched to scientific versimilitude and special effects. The computer-generated SFX elements in particular give the series a quite stunning look.

'The success of *The X-Files* has opened doors for sf series,' says Jed Mercurio, the creator and joint-producer of *Invasion: Earth* who also wrote the original scripts. 'But if they are going to be mainstream dramas, then the production values have got to be strong. We have had the kind of budget to make the programme look very cinematic and that is what we aimed for. If we had been asked to make *Invasion: Earth* for less money and aimed it at the pre-watershed audience, then it would probably have had the look of something like *Bugs*. Instead, I believe we have created a series much closer to *Alien*.'

As something of a landmark, it is also very appropriate that *Invasion: Earth* should be being shown in the centenary year of H. G. Wells's pioneer novel of interplanetary invasion, *The War of the Worlds*. Since its first publication in 1898, the story has been filmed, adapted for radio and television, and utilised in the media in just about every possible form from toys to comic strips. There are other curious links with this classic work which will become evident. (See 'From Mars to Caterham'.)

One of the major locations in *Invasion: Earth* is the Field Headquarters – the nerve centre of the operation set up to prevent the alien attack – a secret base 'somewhere in Scotland'. This highly specialised, computer-driven base where many of the tensest moments are played out represents another example of the film-

Invasion imminent: the front-line team at Kirkhaven (l to r): Major General David Reece, Dr Amanda Tucker, Flight Lieutenant Jim Radcliffe, Group Captain Susan Preston, Flight Lieutenant Christopher Drake and Nick Shay

invasion: earth

makers' wizardry. It was actually created in a disused Army barracks on the edge of the London commuter belt. The reasons for selecting this unlikely spot are explained by joint-producer, Chrissy Skinns.

'Because of the particular demands of the story, we needed a multi-purpose location,' she says. 'We were looking for somewhere that would function as our production base as well as somewhere to construct most of our sets and interiors. The old barracks at Caterham has lots of military-style buildings and proved to be just what we needed. So while we got on with the business of running the production in one building, Rod Stratfold and his design team transformed other bits into an RAF station that had previously been inactive but is brought back on line to deal with the threat from space.'

Terrell's escape pod in Hanger 12 at Field HQ

The Caterham Military Barracks on the Coulsdon Road in Surrey were for years the home of the Coldstream Guards and used as a training base and depot. From here, soldiers were despatched to their regiments, many of them already based in trouble spots all over the world. But as a result of the vision of Rod Stratfold and his team, great areas of the complex were turned into a variety of sets for the production. These included the Operations Room packed with radar equipment, flight plans, maps and computers where the crisis is handled; a high-tech medical unit where some crucial medical experiments and operations are performed; and a Regimental office and living quarters for the servicemen and women. The authenticity of the sets earned special praise from the service personnel brought in to act as advisers on the series.

A row of derelict army houses proved ideal for filming the scenes of the war-torn London of 1944 into which an alien spacecraft plunges at the opening of the story. Nearby, a towering office block formed the exterior for the wartime 'Hospital for Imbeciles' to which the injured extraterrestrial pilot is taken because no one in authority will acknowledge what he is.

To add authenticity to the scenes in which the alien is held in a bare, cell-like room, the production team filmed at the disused Netherne Hospital, not far from Caterham. Some of the most poignant moments of the entire story occur in this episode, during which a reference is made to a most notorious rumour that for years two royal cousins with learning impairments lived out their forlorn lives in just such a place.

Equal care was also taken in selecting a town to represent Kirkhaven, the little Scottish community on which the nDs focus their invasion plans. Here there is less deception than at Caterham – the town is in Scotland, at Dunning in Perthshire (the filming here is described later). Other Scottish locations which were used included RAF Leuchars, RAF Lossiemouth, Aviemore and Loch Ness.

A desire for authenticity runs like a thread through the whole series, both in terms of the scientific *possibility* of the story and the accuracy of the costumes. Howard Burden, the costume designer, had the unique task of re-creating Second World War military uniforms for use alongside futuristic suits for the aliens.

'We worked very closely with the RAF and the MoD right from the beginning to get that aspect of the story correct,' Howard explains. 'We did a lot of research, too, so that everything from the fabric of the civilian clothes to the regimental badges and pips on the uniforms were correct. You don't want anybody ringing up afterwards to tell you such-and-such would not have been worn in the forties. The alien costume was made from a membrane skin so as to give the actor maximum mobility as he had to do so many things from scrambling up rocks to floundering in water. I think every costume in the series looks *believable*.'

The production team – and director of photography, Simon Kossoff, in particular – also took a gamble in deciding to film the Second World War sequences of the story in black and white and at a generally slower pace than the contemporary scenes. There was also controversy over a crucial scene featuring the alien Echoes. In episode one, director Patrick Lau was keen to show Charles Terrell piloting the UFO – Jed Mercurio was not.

Patrick, Jed and Chrissy Skinns talked long and hard about the scene, and in the end they decided to cut it to maintain the mystery of the character.

The special effects provided Jed with a great learning experience, working alongside special effects director, Dennis Lowe. Lowe's mastery of the medium has made the highlight effects of the UFO in flight and the awesome portal in space through which they travel seem wholly authentic.

'As the shoot went on, I became more involved with the SFX,' Jed explains. 'Originally, it would have been the directors working with Dennis and the effects companies, in a very committee-like process. By also getting involved myself I've been able to make a more substantial contribution creatively and financially than by just making the tea or whatever. By the end of it, I think I've become one of the few producers working in TV who is confident about special effects – which will no doubt be good if I do another sf series and make me an even nastier bastard in the process!'

Although violence does occur in the story on a number of occasions, one incident in episode three featuring the alien Echo is of such graphic violence that the production team anticipate protests. It was shot using a prosthetic head and has the same kind of visual impact on the viewer that the creature exploding from John Hurt's stomach in *Alien* did on the big screen. Nicola Buckingham, who played the Echo, had to lie still with a blanket pulled up to her head for many hours while the

Nicola Buckingham being made up as the Echo

scene was being filmed, before handing over to the prosthetic head. The prosthetic head involved looked so real that people on set didn't realise it *wasn't* Nicola, and were actually seen talking to it!

The combination of make-believe and scientific rationale in *Invasion: Earth* has given it an extraordinary appeal – an appeal that may well not end with this series as Jed Mercurio already has plans for a sequel. In the meantime, the realisation of the concept, its science, medicine, alien technology and the factual events that inspired many of the crucial episodes, is the fascinating story that this book has to reveal ...

From Mars to Caterham

By a piece of pure coincidence, the major part of *Invasion: Earth* was filmed in Caterham, Surrey, close to the location of H. G. Wells's classic story of alien invasion, *The War of the Worlds*. Only a few minutes' drive around the M25 from Caterham Barracks lies the town of Woking where the Martian invaders began their onslaught against the unsuspecting men, women and children of southern England.

It was on Horsell Common, just to the west of Woking, that the first alien cylinder landed to establish the beachhead for the reign of terror which threatened to overwhelm the country. In the case of the Martians it was the humble bacteria which came to the rescue of mankind; *Invasion: Earth*'s aliens are, however, of a very different nature.

Wells appears to have been interested in the idea of alien life-forms from his youth. It has been suggested that the first seed of the story was planted in his imagination while he was studying biology in 1887 at the Normal School of Science in London and happened to examine some particularly virulent bacteria under a microscope. Certainly, the following year he addressed the Debating Society at the Royal College of Science on the topic 'Are The Planets Habitable?' and declared that in his opinion, 'there is every reason to suppose that the surface of Mars is occupied by living beings.' Some years later, in April 1896, he published an article in the *Saturday Review*, 'Intelligence on Mars' in which he went even further and said that 'there need not be anything in common between their intelligence and ours.'

However, what gave Wells the real push towards writing *The War of the Worlds* was a chance remark by his brother, Frank, while the two men were walking together through the peaceful Surrey countryside. 'Suppose some beings from another planet were to drop out of the sky suddenly,' Frank Wells exclaimed, 'and began laying about them here!'

An illustration from the original Pearson's Magazine serialisation of The War of the Worlds

invasion: earth

Once Wells had worked out the plot for his story, he knew that something else was just as important if the groundbreaking work was to be acceptable to readers.

'The technical interest of a story like *The War of the Worlds* lies in the attempt to keep everything within the bounds of possibility,' he wrote some years after publication. 'And the value of the story for me lies in this, that from first to last there is nothing in it that is impossible.'

Wells was, though, never in any doubt that he wanted to wreak havoc on the population as Frank had suggested, and admitted as much in a letter to a friend, Elizabeth Healey, in 1896: 'I'm doing the dearest little serial [sic] for Pearson's new magazine in which I completely wreck and destroy Woking,' he wrote, 'killing my neighbours in painful and eccentric ways. Then I proceed via Kingston and Richmond to London, which I sack, selecting South Kensington for feats of peculiar atrocity.'

He also had the idea that one of the invaders' plans was to prey on mankind, particularly those who lead indolent and wasted lives. His character, the Artilleryman – clearly reflecting his own views – says of them: 'Well, the Martians will just be a god-send to these. Nice roomy cages, fattening food, careful breeding, no worry.'

Wells was one of the earliest writers to describe widespread panic in the face of fear of the unknown. This has since proved to be one of the enduring themes of twentieth century science fiction, and one exploited again in *Invasion: Earth*. The exodus of people from London – with the cries of the police ringing in their ears, 'They are coming! The Martians are coming!' – provides one of the great descriptions of mass hysteria in literature.

It is the credibility of the story of *The War of the Worlds* with its recognisable locations and ordinary people caught up in the most extraordinary events, that have made it such a compelling piece of writing. The commonplace description of Horsell Bridge coupled with an account of the nightmare figures of the Martians moving across the Woking countryside make them both seem equally real in the reader's imagination. The fact that the book is told in the first person and narrated in an almost documentary style completes the overwhelming feeling of authenticity. Even today, a reader can half-expect to hear the crunch of the invaders in the distance as he turns the pages of the book.

Whatever reasons Wells may have had for writing his masterpiece – other than telling a very good story – there can be no doubt about its lasting influence on science fiction. The excitement of the first encounter with the aliens as the cylinder unscrews, the vivid description of the destruction of parts of Surrey, and the unforgettable horrors of dead and abandoned London remain long in the memory. It is the same kind of images that *Invasion: Earth* has created a century later: not on the printed page but in a medium that was unknown in Wells' day – television.

The Search for E. T.

The attempt to establish contact with alien intelligence which so absorbs Dr Amanda Tucker and Nick Shay in *Invasion: Earth* is their contribution to a continuing worldwide investigation known as SETI – The Search for Extraterrestrial Intelligence. Nick, the young whiz-kid computer expert who wrote his Ph.D. under Amanda's supervision on 'The Radio Search for Extraterrestrial Intelligence', believes that trying to talk to aliens 'is potentially the biggest thing in history'. It is a view shared by a band of international astronomers and scientists all linked by SETI.

When Nick sits in front of his computer screen in episode one and taps out the words 'Notification to Central Bureau for Astronomical Telegrams of the International Astronomical Union', he believes he has confirmed the dream of countless other searchers that there *is* life out there. (The IAU has had a permanent committee for SETI since the early 1980s and has received hundreds of reports.) But before he can send his message: URGENT SETI REPORT – RECEIPT OF SIGNAL OF SUSPECTED EXTRATERRESTRIAL ORIGIN, Amanda angrily demands that he delete it. The signal may indeed have been from an alien, she agrees, but she wants no one to know until they have found out what it actually *says* . . .

Although mankind has been debating for centuries about the possibility of life on other planets, it was only in 1975 that a systematic search for other life-forms in space was proposed under the auspices of the National Aeronautics and Space Administration (NASA) following a series of meetings held at the Ames Research Centre in the USA. The scientists and astronomers who were brought together at these workshops began by considering earlier attempts to discover if there was life in the universe.

The investigators also reviewed the contemporary evidence that of the many millions of stars in our galaxy, there was a fraction with planets surrounding them like our sun and these *could* harbour life. But how to make contact with these cosmic cousins? If there was a practicable and already available way of reaching them – in whatever form they might exist – then powerful radio telescopes able to sweep the vast reaches of space were probably the most likely route to success. If there was intelligent life out there, the researchers agreed, then these beings would surely be sophisticated enough to have developed radio communications, and as a result of reaching out to them, one day they might return a message to us here on Earth.

In the years which followed the meetings at the Ames Research Centre, only a great yawning silence greeted the scientists' best endeavours as radio telescopes were mobilised to scan the heavens. With the one exception, that is, picked up at Ohio State

invasion: earth

University and referred to in SETI history as the 'Wow Signal'. The sound, which remains unexplained to this day, was monitored by a researcher who could only think to write the word, 'Wow' on his printout and thereby gave the mystery its popular name.

But those like Dr Tucker and Nick Shay who search for the evidence that we are not alone, have persevered in their investigations. Apart from the NASA project, in 1984 a privately-funded SETI Institute was opened at Mountain View in California and attracted patronage from the world's leading astronomers. The huge success of the Steven Speilberg movie, *E.T.* in 1982 also generated fresh public interest in the idea of finding a real alien to call. Dr David Whitehouse, a NASA consultant on SETI, was quoted in the press on this very theme:

'Although we are looking for life similar to our own, we may in the words of *Star Trek*'s Mr Spock, come across "life not as we know it now". But just as we are looking for other life-forms, somebody out there could be looking for us. Our civilisation is a very young one, and the probability is that any aliens would be from a much more advanced and ancient civilisation. They may well find us before we find *them*.'

Of late, the SETI Institute has been busy running Project Hermes from the Parkes Observatory in Australia and has so far studied in detail over 200 stars. The President of the Institute is Frank Drake, Professor of Astronomy and Astrophysics at the University of California, and the man who in 1960 first began to look for extraterrestrial signals at the National Radio Astronomy Observatory in West Virginia (in what he called Project Ozma after the princess in the *Wizard of Oz* books). Although he found nothing, Drake was still pleased. 'For all we knew then, every star in the sky had a booming civilisation,' he says today. 'It would have been foolish *not* to look.'

Professor Drake is revered in the field as the inventor of the 'Drake Equation', a complex formula which sets out to prove that of the 100 billion stars in the galaxy, a total of 1,000 probably have civilisations at least as advanced as our own. To radio astronomers everywhere, he is the father of SETI.

The Professor believes that new advances in technology are bringing the day when we make contact with aliens ever closer. 'Years ago we used to look at a hundred different frequencies simultaneously, but now that figure is closer to a billion. Of course, another civilisation may transmit messages in some other way, but imagine the rewards if we do find something?'

Drake, along with a number of other scientists, believes that any kind of complex message would probably come in two parts. 'A message with a high information content is more difficult to detect,' he says. 'That's due to the law of physics – it's not something we can overcome with technology. So if another civilisation wants to enrich the galaxy with its knowledge, the communication will probably involve two separate messages. The first is called the beacon, and it tells you where to tune in to get the second message. The beacon is a sort of signpost, telling you where the public library is. The second – the library – you could call the information channel.'

Another equally ambitious project has also come into existence at the University of California at Berkeley with the delightful title, SERENDIP. This stands for the Search for Extraterrestrial Radio Emissions from Nearby Developed Intelligent Populations. It almost sounds like an invention of its chairman, the doyen of sci-fi writers, Arthur C. Clarke, except for the fact it is using the world's biggest radio telescope, the 1,000 foot dish of the Arecibo Observatory in Puerto Rico, for its enquiries.

The project manager of SERENDIP is Dan Werthimer who accepts that while other civilisations may have infinitely superior technologies to ours, radio remains the best option for making contact. 'It travels at the speed of light,' he explains, 'so it's the fastest thing we have and it doesn't use up much energy. And because this is such an important question, we have to start somewhere.'

Some astronomers and physicists have speculated that advanced civilisations would probably use neutrinos (fast-moving, subatomic particles so light that they may have no mass) or gravity waves (slight, wave-like undulations in the curvature of space) for making interstellar contact.

The pictures of fossilised material collected on a space mission to Mars that NASA released in August 1996, hailed in some quarters as proof that life may once have existed on the planet, were greeted by Dan Werthimer with guarded optimism. 'If there does turn out to have been life on Mars, it would show that life started independently on two planets in our solar system. That would mean that there probably *is* tons of life out there.'

The SETI Institute and SERENDIP have now got British scientists and astronomers involved in their search for extraterrestrial life with the recent decision of the scientists at Jodrell Bank in Cheshire to link in with the 250 foot Lovell telescope. Dr Richard Davis, who is in charge of the project in the UK, says: 'I believe we now have a system that's up to the job. If there are any transmissions out there, we'll find them.' Interestingly, both of the American organisations are convinced that contact with aliens presents no likelihood of an attack. Their two leading lights have been specifically quoted on the matter.

Professor Frank Drake, for his part, believes there is a practical reason why such an invasion could not occur. 'Any aliens would need to travel at a great deal faster than the speed of light to reach here. The energy needed to do this would far exceed any resources we can offer. It seems to me that the laws of physics and the distances between the stars conspire so that we can only be friends.'

Dan Werthimer is even more certain. 'We don't really have anything the aliens would want – so I'm not worried about them coming to eat us.'

Invasion: Earth, of course, has a *very* different theory to offer on this subject …

the BATTLE for EARTH

*Previous page:
nD emerging from
a portal*

The idea for *Invasion: Earth* evolved from a very simple premise: *What would happen if the RAF shot down a UFO?* Reports of strange objects in the sky and accounts of alleged encounters with aliens are nowadays almost commonplace. It could be just a matter of time until a spacecraft is tracked entering a nation's airspace where, because it cannot be identified or its purpose established, it prompts the ultimate action from a fighter pilot. The sovereignty of the air above any country has been jealously guarded almost since the birth of flight and this has resulted in a number of headline-making incidents when foreign aircraft have, mostly accidentally, intruded into a nation's airspace. But what when the craft is not of this earth?

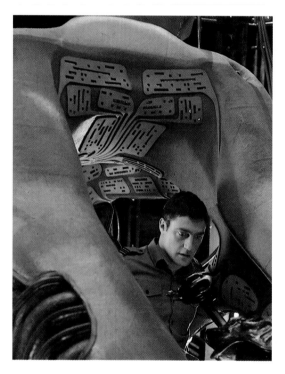

*Flight Lieutenant
Drake (Vincent
Regan) sits in the
pilot's seat of the
alien escape pod*

This was the idea that came into the mind of producer Jed Mercurio a couple of years ago and — like UFOs themselves — refused to go away. A quietly-spoken man whose laid-back approach belies a fierce determination, Jed remembers well the moment of inspiration which has now become a six-part television series.

'I was working in Scotland at the time and there was a lot of talk about a place called Bonnybridge,' Jed recalls. 'There had been this flap going on there for years about UFOs and no one had an adequate explanation of what it was all about. That started me thinking and I asked myself: What if UFOs are real? I read up on Bonnybridge and UFOs in general and gradually an idea began to take shape in my head.' (See 'The Bonnybridge Triangle'.) Its influence on Jed can be seen in the early drafts of the script, where the Scottish town which is the focus of the alien invasion was actually called Oakbridge. The place was only renamed Kirkhaven in mid-August 1997 after shooting had begun.

Although Jed Mercurio's introduction to television actually came through working on a medical drama, *Cardiac Arrest*, from 1994–1996, he has been interested in science fiction films since his childhood. He explains:

'When I was a kid I really liked the old *Star Trek* series which I started watching on television in the mid-seventies. They were also showing the classic old science fiction films like *The Day The Earth Stood Still*, *Invasion of the Body Snatchers* and *Forbidden Planet* which is by far my favourite. Then came *Star Wars* in 1977 which was a terrific success and the cinema began to rediscover science fiction. Sf movies became 'A' list rather than 'B' list features.

'One success followed another. There was *Alien* – which I didn't actually see at the cinema because I was too young to get in – followed by *Predator*, the Terminator films and, of course, the various *Alien* sequels which I was able to watch! So you can see from a pretty early age I have taken my influences from the cinema and television. I'm not a great reader of sf – in fact, I'm not a great reader at all.'

Jed acknowledges another landmark influence on his work: the hugely popular US series about the paranormal, *The X-Files*.

'*The X-Files* has not influenced me creatively, but commercially. I believe there is a lot we can learn from its success about not patronising your audience. I think it has shown a lot of TV executives that science fiction can be mainstream drama. It doesn't have to be marginalised as something for children and put in an early evening slot, or even shunted away on BBC 2. *The X-Files* has done a tremendous amount to raise the whole consciousness of people towards science fiction on television.'

Jed is actually a qualified doctor and worked for two years in the NHS before his urge to write for television took over.

'I started writing scripts while I was still practising,' he reflects. 'Working in medicine presents you with so many good ideas for stories that I thought it was time someone wrote a series from the inside. It wasn't altogether a new idea considering that hospital dramas have been one of the staples of television ever since *Emergency Ward Ten*, but I thought I could write something that was more technically based as well as being entertaining.'

The result was *Cardiac Arrest*, a hospital drama that showed medicine warts and all. It was often cynical in its depiction of hospital staff, but mixed humour with drama and earned its fair share of controversy during the three seasons it ran under its producers, Margaret Matheson and Paddy Higson. The stars were Helen Baxendale and Jo Dow who played Dr James Mortimer, a gay anaesthetist suffering from AIDS. He has returned to life in *Invasion: Earth* playing a very different role as the no-nonsense Flight Lieutenant Jim Radcliffe.

Jed refers to the series today with tongue-in-cheek as a 'socio-realistic revisionist drama of hospital life', but remains understandably proud of it.

'*Cardiac Arrest* was the first series of its kind to have lots of medical jargon in it. In fact this has now become the norm. I like to deal with things that are technical in my writing – partly because I'm too lazy to do the research on relationships! No, I stick to medical and scientific things because I have always had a general interest in science and there are elements of physics and maths which I dimly remember from my 'A' levels. Most of my confident writing is about medicine and technology in one form or another.'

Overleaf: Work on Terrell's escape pod in the hangar

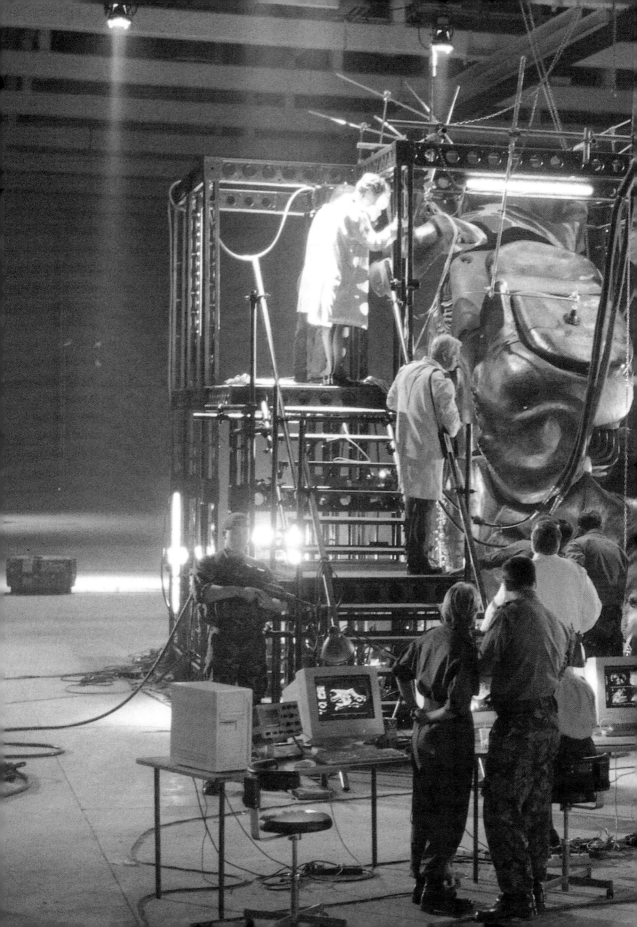

Working on *Cardiac Arrest* gave Jed inside knowledge of how a TV series is put together. He also learned that actors fluffing lines and props going astray were not the only problems to be coped with if and when he became a producer himself. He particularly remembers an incident when the first assistant director accidentally electrocuted himself with a defibrillator. It was the first serious incident on a set he had seen, and it has made him take particular care when using technical equipment – and it's made him make sure there are experts around to give instruction to the actors using them.

The success of the series also convinced Jed that he had a future in the television industry rather than in the NHS. But what to do next?

'Because of my interest in science fiction I knew that I wanted to do something of the kind at some point in my career, but I never imagined it was going to happen the way it did. The success of *The X-Files* meant all of a sudden there was a real market for it and there were lots of people in television talking about doing a science fiction show. I was approached by the BBC to become involved in writing some episodes for projects they had in development, but that very quickly turned into the idea of me doing my own show.'

Interestingly, what Jed initially had in mind was very different to the *Invasion: Earth* which has reached the screen.

'The first outline I did was called *Ten Thousand Light Years From Home*. It was basically the story of the pilot of a UFO who crashes and how he tries to get back home. It was a kind of "pilot crashes behind enemy lines" sort of thing. I did it that way because the show was seen as a half-hour programme for kids on BBC 2. And for a time I rolled with that.

'But then I came back with an hour-long, big-budget, post-watershed outline which the BBC liked. People began to see the story as a mainstream drama. That was the first battle to be won. Having written one episode, I was asked where the story would go then and I really didn't know. So they asked me to think about it and write another episode. So I just went where the story led me. And when I delivered the script, Andrea Calderwood, the Head of Drama at BBC Scotland, immediately saw the idea as a six-parter and gave the green light. She then became involved as Executive Producer of the series, and if she hadn't I can tell you *Invasion: Earth* would have been a very different kind of show.'

As soon as Jed's idea went into development, Gareth Neame, the original joint-producer, Andrea Calderwood and Jed decided to bring in a number of other writers to contribute ideas for the storyline. This is common practice in television and among those who contributed to the widening of the basic plotline from the adventures of a crashed UFO pilot to an intergalactic struggle for the future of the

Earth were Stephen Baxter, Alex Stewart, Paul Mars and Geoff Povey. Meanwhile, Gareth Neame left to develop single dramas, and Chrissy Skinns came on board as joint-producer. A script editor, Ruth McCance, was also assigned to the project at about the same time as Chrissy joined. Ruth, Chrissy and Jed then formed a creative triumvirate and the other writers left.

This editorial team helped the story to move on a lot, and the script development was an organic process as people came on board. It became a kind of committee where Jed would bring ideas, and the rest of the team would come back with their thoughts as to whether something would work or might need some explanation. The storyline grew out of this process, until Jed wrote the finished shooting scripts that went before the cameras.

Apart from the stories of UFOs at Bonnybridge, Jed was also aware of the even more famous events that had occurred at Roswell in New Mexico in 1947. A space ship was said to have crashed in the desert with an alien crew whose bodies were found in the wreckage, the facts of which were immediately suppressed by the authorities. (See 'The Roswell Incident'.)

'When I started writing *Invasion: Earth* I thought about what had happened at Roswell and maybe using the events as the starting point of the story. I looked at the facts and wondered why there had been so much about *if* it had happened, while nobody had tried to explain *why*. So as a dramatist you aim to find reasons why something is motivated and look at the consequences. I took the incident and asked myself *what* would motivate an alien race to go to Roswell and *why* would they crash? I actually came up with what I thought was a passable explanation, but at the same time I also began to realise that perhaps the whole thing was becoming a bit old hat. I could just hear people saying, "Oh, no, not *that* again!"'

Jed decided the story needed a British angle. One obvious and well authenticated story of rockets crash-landing on Britain were the German V-1 and V-2 weapons which had caused such terrible damage to London and the south-east of England between 1944–1945. (See 'The German V-Rockets'.)

Initially, the suggestion was that the story might begin on the German island of Peenamunde where the flying bombs were developed. But that was quickly switched to 1940s London which the production team agreed offered much more potential.

'I was immediately intrigued with exploring the idea of an alien space ship crash-landing amongst all those German rockets,' says Jed. 'What would people make of it – especially if it was a bomb disposal unit who found it? Once I had the idea it seemed perfect and I also found I could come back to it later in the story and tie everything together. Again it was quite organic. I was attracted to the idea dramatically, and it offered something that was visually interesting because of the period.'

As a result of this, it was decided to shoot the opening sequence of the series when the ship crashes and its crew are discovered in the rubble of an air raid in black and white. Some early film trial tests were made using sepia, but the production team decided these lacked the stark, dramatic edge of black and white.

But where to film a scene that looked like war-torn London half a century ago? There were no longer any derelict sites from the war still in London and to wreck a street just for filming would obviously be prohibitively expensive. Luck smiled on the production team when Rod Stratfold spotted a group of bedraggled old houses from the period standing right beside the barracks in Caterham. These required some further work by the art department, and with the help of some special effects doubled perfectly as a row of bombed buildings surrounded by the rubble of an air raid. The firing of some of the houses and the addition of a vehicle on fire completed the effect which looked all the more authentic in black and white – as well as providing a nostalgic moment for viewers old enough to have lived through the real thing.

invasion: earth

Colour stock, lit and graded as black and white, was used for shooting almost a third of episode three when the origin of the occupants of the UFO becomes evident. Both of these sequences have much of the look and atmosphere of a wartime cinema newsreel.

This aspect of *Invasion: Earth* also harks back forty years to one of the most famous of the BBC's television science fiction serials, *Quatermass and the Pit*, which was shown entirely in black and white during the winter of 1958. The production was the third in a series written by the actor turned screenwriter, Nigel Kneale, that had begun in 1953 with *The Quatermass Experiment*, and which the BBC announced beforehand was considered 'unsuitable for children or persons of a nervous disposition.' The story featured an astronaut who returns to earth infected by spores from space that turn him into an amorphous blob which the redoubtable Professor Quatermass (Reginald Tate) causes to self-destruct in Westminster Abbey. It proved to be a milestone in televised science fiction.

Work going on outside the houses in Caterham which provided the backdrop for the crash of the alien spacecraft during World War Two

invasion: earth

33

An Army bomb disposal team investigate the alien aircraft in Quatermass and the Pit.

Two years later *Quatermass II* was transmitted. This was about an alien invasion of the north of England to exploit ordinary people which could only be stopped by Quatermass (now played by John Robinson) going into space to destroy an asteroid; it, too, was considered a very adventurous production for the time. *Quatermass and the Pit*, shown in 1958, was perhaps the best of the series. In this story, workers carrying out reconstruction in one of the last blitzed areas of London, find what looks like an unexploded bomb and call in the bomb disposal unit. Their leader, Captain Potter (John Stratton) is the first to suspect it may not be a bomb at all, and aided by the ubiquitous Professor (Andre Morrell at the top of his form), the two men discover it is actually a Martian space ship with its dead crew still aboard. The excavation site (complete with the space ship) where much of the action took place was actually created with tons of mud by designer Clifford Hatts, in what was then the BBC's newly acquired Ealing studios. According to popular legend, while this series was on air, pubs and clubs across the land emptied for each episode. The parallels between the early scenes in war-torn London in Jed Mercurio's story and the activities of the bomb disposal men in Nigel Kneale's will not be lost on those who have seen both.

A fourth story which Kneale wrote in the late sixties, *The Quatermass Conclusion*, about hippies being lured to neolithic sites by aliens, was rejected by the BBC as being too expensive and was not made until 1979 by Euston Films for ITV, starring John Mills and produced by Ted Childs.

Later series like *Blake's 7* and *Doctor Who* were always made as science fiction instead of drama, and these lost out in terms of audience ratings and time-slots. It is something of a tragedy that having produced milestones of television science fiction such as *Quatermass*, it has taken forty years for the BBC to once again consider it as a mainstream in-house drama in the form of *Invasion: Earth*.

The Bonnybridge Triangle

Bonnybridge, not far from Falkirk in the central belt of Scotland is an unprepossessing little industrial town whose delightful name belies its everyday appearance. Yet this is the place where a unique series of events which have occurred since the early nineties helped to inspire the story of *Invasion: Earth*.

Situated beside the old Forth and Clyde Canal the small community has made little impact on the history of Scotland since the days when the Roman fort of Rough Castle was built. This strategically-placed earthworks, consisting of a large fort and the remains of a ditch and ramparts in wooded surroundings, has been called one of the most notable Roman military sites in Britain. Until recently, it was the only real tourist attraction the town could boast.

However, during the past six years Bonnybridge has become famous in a quite unexpected way. It has been the location of more recorded sightings of UFOs than anywhere else in Britain. Between 1992 and 1994 alone, over 8,000 reports were made by local inhabitants. In such a spot, whose only previous claim to a curiosity was an allegedly haunted copse of trees known as Seabegs Wood, it has come as much of a surprise to the local residents as the rest of the world. Now stories of mysterious lights in the sky have taken over from the tales of ghostly invaders who are believed to haunt the vicinity of the wood.

The phenomena, which have come to be known in some quarters as 'The Bonnybridge Triangle', began with a series of strange lights which were seen in the night sky. Naturally hesitant about discussing anything out of the ordinary, it was only when these lights became more recognisable as objects of some kind that local people started to believe something strange might be going on. The obvious explanations of aircraft passing overhead or tricks of the light just did not fit the increasing number of reports.

When the reports from Bonnybridge were collated, a picture emerged of saucer-shaped objects with bright orange or blue lights that hovered in the sky over the town before speeding off into the distance. A few accounts even spoke of a 'huge, triangular-shaped craft' which terrified everyone who saw it.

Such was the local interest, that town councillor Billy Buchanan called a public meeting to discuss the sightings. Media attended from all over the world – including American and Japanese TV camera crews – but curiously the British press was noticeable by its absence. Mr Buchanan thereafter found himself acting as spokesman for the townspeople as well as producing his own eye-witness account of events, *The Lights of Bonnybridge*. He has also written to the Government urging them to launch a full-scale enquiry into the mystery.

invasion: earth

'There is no doubt there is something out there,' he says. 'There have been so many sightings there just has to be. On the one hand it is quite unnerving, but there is no doubt about the interest it has caused. I have had visitors from all over the world wanting to know about the UFOs. It has got to the point where there isn't enough accommodation for them.'

Theories as to the cause of the UFOs abound in Bonnybridge – beyond their being extraterrestrial in origin. Ley-lines are favoured by some local people, as is an idea that they may somehow be caused by the old Roman wall at Seabegs Wood. Certainly, by night, this is a place where *anything* could happen . . .

The Roswell Incident

The extraordinary events which occurred near the town of Roswell in New Mexico in the summer of 1947 are still considered to be the most controversial account of a so-called alien spacecraft to crash-land on Earth. The facts, such as they are, were originally to be featured in *Invasion: Earth*, but instead provided the inspiration for the story in episode one when a crashed UFO escape pod is discovered in Scotland and spirited away by the RAF for inspection.

It was during the night of 2 July 1947, as a fierce storm raged across New Mexico, that a rancher named William 'Mac' Brazel living on the outskirts of Roswell was suddenly awoken by a loud explosion. The appalling weather persuaded him against making an immediate investigation, but the following morning he was up and out early to investigate the mystery. What he found lying scattered on the ground nearby were some very strange pieces of debris.

As Brazel examined the wreckage in the morning sunlight, he noticed that the bits were not only very shiny and metallic, but feather-light and pliable, almost like balsa wood, though a great deal stronger. When he took the debris back to his house, he was quite unable to dent it with even the hardest blow of a sledgehammer. Most curious of all, he saw that the wreckage bore several strange symbols of a kind he had never seen before.

William Brazel's first thoughts were that perhaps the material was the remains of an aircraft from the nearby Roswell Air Base, which he knew to be the station of the US's only atomic bomber squadron and a site where secret research into rocketry was being carried out. So he telephoned the military with his discovery. Later that day, an Intelligence Officer, Major Jesse Marcel, and a team of USAF personnel came out to the ranch and collected all the bits of wreckage they could find and took them back to the airbase for examination.

invasion: earth

A press release from the Air Base later that same day seemed to confirm that 'Flying Saucers' were, after all, real. The wreckage, it said, had come from a UFO, and the bits were now being flown to the Wright Patterson Air Force Base in Dayton, Ohio, for closer inspection. Within twenty-four hours, however, the story had changed dramatically. According to a second statement, the object had only been a metal fabric weather balloon which had been brought down in the storm. The whole incident had been a case of mistaken identity – this became the official line – and newspaper photographers were allowed to take pictures of the material – though from a distance.

Within a matter of days, the 'Roswell Incident' had disappeared from the front pages of the newspapers and would probably have remained forgotten but for the unshakable conviction of Major Jesse Marcel about what he had seen – plus the dogged investigations of a number of UFO researchers who were far from satisfied by the statement of the authorities. To the end of his life, Marcel continued to insist: 'That debris was something I had never seen before or since – it certainly wasn't anything built by us or the Russians.'

The UFO researchers' persistent enquiries among the people of Roswell also pointed to the weather balloon story being a hastily-concocted invention to cover the real facts. The wreckage from the desert certainly *did* go to Ohio – but seemingly alarmed by what the scientists there discovered, the more commonplace and less controversial version of events was issued. In the years since 1947, gossip, rumour and legend have been busy with the Roswell Incident.

According to the most popular story, an alien craft *did* crash in New Mexico on July 2 and later a lot more debris was found on the desert terrain and taken for storage to the Wright Patterson base. More remarkable still, the bodies of several alien crew members were also recovered during this search. Since then, a variety of documents – including an extraordinary piece of film claiming to show one of the alien corpses – have been produced to 'prove' that both the craft and the bodies are still being kept in a secure facility where scientists have been endeavouring to unlock the secret of the alien visitors. The extraordinary tale has also generated numerous books including *Majestic* by Whitley Strieber, the movie *Hanger 18*, and material for popular TV series such as *The Twilight Zone* and *The X-Files*.

The mystery of the Roswell Incident is far from over, however. Arguments still continue to rage over what *did* happen that stormy night. Certainly, if the aliens' intention was to warn the Earth of the dangers of atomic experimentation – as some writers have suggested – there could have been no better place to come: the first atom bombs had been tested nearby just two years earlier. In fact, some highly classified and potentially devastating experiments were even then taking place. On the other hand, the US itself might just have been trying out a top secret aircraft, details of which – perhaps due to its failure – have never been made public.

Recently, new evidence concerning the UFO crash has been presented to the Roswell Museum which has a section devoted to the events. According to the *San Antonio Express News* of 29 March 1996, a mysterious piece of a metallic substance covered with intricate lines has been donated to the museum by a local resident. Although the man insisted that his identity was to be kept a secret, the curator, Max Littel, told the newspaper: 'From the information we have, the material is from a guy who was stationed here and was part of the crew that helped to pick up the debris. We are not saying one way or the other if this is actually a piece of a space ship, but we will do everything we can to find out.'

The German V-Rockets

The German high-explosive V-rockets which fall on London in the opening sequence of *Invasion: Earth* brought terror and death to the people of the capital during the last year of the Second World War. From June 1944 until March 1945, Hitler's *Vergeltungswaffe*, or 'Revenge Weapons', the V-1 and V-2, rained down on southern England in a nightly blitz made all the more terrible by the sound of wailing sirens and the sight of waving searchlights as the defence forces tried desperately to stem the tide of flying bombs.

The suggestion in episode three when two alien bodies are found in a UFO that this might be a third type of V-weapon actually being *piloted* by recruits of the Luftwaffe – perhaps freaks or imbeciles from the labour camps – is, remarkably, not without its basis in fact. German scientists had already begun trials in April of that year with a converted V-1, known as the R-1 or *Reichenberg*, which was to be flown against England by suicide pilots when all else had failed. The men are mistaken, although it takes Lieutenant Charles Terrell (Anton Lesser), the officer who plays such a crucial role in the story of *Invasion: Earth* to suspect the extraterrestrial origins of the two beings in the escape pod. But the R-1 might just have become a reality.

The first of the weapons, the V-1, (or *Flakzielgerat 76* – 'Anti-aircraft Aiming Device 76' – to give it the official German classification, intended to deceive Allied intelligence analysts as to its true purpose) appeared over the skies of London on 13 June 1944. A mid-wing monoplane pilotless aircraft with a wing-span of 16 feet and an overall length of 25 feet, it had been launched from occupied France and fell on Grove Road, Bow. The explosion killed six people.

The missiles – which can be seen as an early version of today's Cruise missiles – had as their power unit a pulse-jet consisting of a modified Argus duct. The V-1s ran on half a ton of low-grade aviation fuel and the motor would continue to function for between 30 to 60 minutes. In flight, they made a sound which one English eyewitness described as 'a disagreeable splutter, like an aerial motor cycle in bad running order.'

Though these flying bombs were easy enough to hear and not too difficult to see because they flew low, it was the sound of the motor cutting out as it reached its maximum theoretical range of 160 miles (later models could reach 250 miles) that signalled 'the deafening silence of doom.' For then the V-1 with its ton of high explosives in the warhead would be on a 12-second plunge to earth before detonating on impact. As long as they could be heard, it was said, you were safe.

In time, it was learned that these 'aerial torpedoes' or 'doodlebugs' were not radio-controlled as had at first been thought, but launched from 150 foot long steam catapult ramps in the Pas de Calais near Dieppe and on the Cherbourg peninsula, by means of a propulsive device (Dampferzeuger) which made use of the powerful reaction between hydrogen peroxide and permanganate of potash. Once heading towards its target, the V-1 would turn on to a course pre-set on a magnetic compass that monitored the automatic pilot. After a spinning propeller in the nose cone had completed a predetermined number of revolutions, a tachometer would switch on an electro-mechanical device which swung the explosive missile into a dive. A number of doodlebugs were later released from specially modified Heinkel III aircraft. Of the 10,500 V-1s aimed at the UK in 1944 and 1945, a total of about 1,600 were launched from aircraft and the remaining 8,900 from ramps on the French coast.

The V-2 weapon which was the forerunner of the moon rocket

  invasion: earth

At the height of the German V-1 attacks on England, as many as 100 of the 'malignant robots' (as the Ministry of Defence liked to call them) appeared in the skies each day, some falling harmlessly in fields, but others more devastatingly on the crowded streets of London. The anti-aircraft gunners on the ground did their best to bring down the missiles. But flying at over 400 mph this was not an easy task, and the balloon barrage which had been raised to keep away enemy planes proved easy for the tiny machines to slip past. Only RAF pilots flying the newest fighters like the Tempest had a real chance of catching them in the air.

The German scientists and technicians led by Walter Dornberger and Dr Wernher von Braun who had helped in the development of the V-1 from their secret research centre on the Baltic island of Peenemunde soon had ready an even more deadly weapon to launch at the unsuspecting enemy. And on the evening of September 8 at about 6.43 pm, the first of the awesome V-2 long-range rockets plunged down in Chiswick, west London, killing three people and seriously injuring nineteen. At the same time an identical rocket fell to the north in fields near the market town of Epping in Essex, without causing any casualties.

Although the V-2 also carried a ton of explosives, that was where the similarity with its predecessor ended. It stood 46 feet tall, could be launched from mobile transporters, and travelled to a height of 60 miles at a speed in excess of 3,600 mph. There was no defence that could withstand the V-2, Nazi propaganda at once began to boast. A sinister double thunderclap and then a sudden bright flash which lit up the sky were to be all that anyone in England would know of the weapon – *after* it had struck its target.

The V-2, or *Aggregate-4* in German terminology was, in fact, a gyroscopically-stabilised finned rocket which weighed just under four tons and had a warhead containing 1,650 lbs of explosives. Its diameter around the middle was nearly five-and-a-half feet and this carried four tons of a three-to-one mixture of ethyl alcohol and water and about five tons of liquid oxygen, which gave it an all-out weight at take-off of almost 13 tons. The V-2 was launched in the upright position, the fuel and oxidant being forced into the combustion chamber by powerful pumps using relatively small quantities of hydrogen peroxide and permanganate. It reached the speed of sound in just 30 seconds.

The minimum range of this deadly new weapon was between 200 to 250 miles, and once it had reached the peak of its predetermined trajectory it was moving at 3,600 mph. This speed then declined to between 2,500–2,200 mph at the moment of impact with its target. The course of the V-2 was governed by the set of vanes at the rear of the fins pre-set to the calculated line of shoot. Some versions could also be controlled by a radio beam during the early stages of flight, or alternately by using an integrating accelerometer in the rocket which was pre-set to turn off the fuel and cause it to tilt progressively downwards.

Before the Allied forces finally overran the German positions in France and Holland, the last V-2 was fired from the Hague and landed at Orpington in Kent on 27 March 1945. A total of 1,403 of these rocket weapons, the world's first long-range ballistic missiles – which might so easily have turned the tide of war if they had become operational earlier – were launched, killing 2,754 people, before Hitler's campaign of *Vergeltungswaffe* ended. Together the V-1 and V-2 had cost the lives of almost ten thousand British civilians and injured in excess of twenty-five thousand.

The third of the V-weapons, the piloted version, thankfully never reached England. Intended to be virtually a suicide bomb, the Fieseler 103R-IV, codenamed *Reichenberg*, was conceived by the Germans long before the first Japanese Kamikaze aircraft plunged on to the American fleet in Leyte Gulf on 25 October 1944. This new version of the V-1 looked very like the original, except that a seat for the pilot was fitted in place of one of the globes containing compressed air which was no longer needed to operate the controls automatically. The pilot was to fly the R-rocket on its one-way mission with the most rudimentary controls: a joystick, foot-operated rudder bar joined to the skids and flaps, plus an airspeed indicator, altimeter and clock. Its great advantage over both its predecessors was that it could be steered *accurately* to its target. However, none were ever actually flown.

According to a directive issued by Himmler who was a great supporter of the project, the pilots 'should be recruited among the incurably diseased, the neurotics, and the criminals so that through a voluntary death they might redeem their "honour" ' – words echoed in *Invasion: Earth* by Major Alex Friedkin to Charles Terrell when disputing the origin of the machine in the London ruins.

Out of all this death and tragedy, however, came the birth of the Space Age. At the end of the war, the US Army took home enough pieces to recreate nearly 80 of the rockets plus a group of German scientists led by Walter Dornberger and Wernher von Braun to work on Project Hermes. Subsequently, over 60 V-2s were launched from the White Sands Proving Ground in New Mexico during the late 1940s and early Fifties. These once-deadly weapons stripped of their explosives provided the first practical experience with large rockets in the United States. They also formed the basis for later US advances in the exploration of space, the launching of scientific instruments above the atmosphere and, finally, the giant Saturn V rocket which in July 1969 launched astronaut Neil Armstrong in Apollo 11 on his epic voyage from Cape Canaveral to the surface of the moon.

UFO
Alert!

In the event of a UFO alert in the skies over Britain, the RAF would certainly be at the forefront of the action. Fighter aircraft would be scrambled to intercept the unidentified object and establish whether it was friend or foe, and, if possible, its point of origin. The procedure is one that the service has not *officially* admitted to ever having carried out. But there are those both inside and outside the RAF who believe the same tactics would be employed as if the intruder was thought to belong to a hostile nation.

One of the most powerful elements of *Invasion: Earth* is the authenticity of the flying sequences throughout the story. Particularly impressive are the scenes of pilots from 313 Fighter Squadron's base near the east coast of Scotland being dispatched to investigate reported UFO sightings over the country and the North Sea. The workings of a front-line fighter station, the hive of activity in the hangers, and the stark roar of jets taking off from the runways are all presented with great verisimilitude which owes much to the skill of the director and camera crews, and to Wing Commander Bernard Grant, the project officer who worked to help the whole team get the shots they needed.

Jed Mercurio also had some inside knowledge crucial to the creation of the series. He might, in fact, have become one of the fighter pilots he describes in the story of *Invasion: Earth* rather than a qualified doctor. Jed actually trained to be a pilot alongside studying for a career in medicine and ultimately becoming a writer and producer of TV series.

Jed was a student at Birmingham University when he joined the University Air Squadron and, sponsored by the RAF, learned to fly. As a Pilot Officer, he put in 150 hours of flying on various types of aircraft, including 20 hours on a Hawk jet trainer based at RAF Valley.

'I toyed with the idea of a career in the RAF for some time,' he recalls, 'but it never quite worked out. I qualified for military flying, but never became fully operational in any way. Which was a pity, because I did want to be a pilot. But what I learned during that time has been very useful in scripting and filming *Invasion: Earth*.'

The flying sequences in the series are among some of the best to have been seen on television in recent years. The combination of studio shots of a cockpit coupled with on-the-spot film of take-offs and landings, plus highly authentic SFX sequences of planes in flight, has earned the production team compliments from the series' RAF advisers.

Apart from the knowledge he had gained as an RAF Officer, Jed also checked many of the facts in the story with the Ministry of Defence whom he found remarkably co-operative. They talked to him in detail about the scripts which they

Left: Radcliffe (Jo Dow) and Drake (Vincent Regan) inside a Chinook helicopter

Below: Tornado F3 at RAF Leuchars

were, in general, quite happy with. They especially liked the tone of the series and its accurate portrayal of the RAF.

'As far as I was able to establish there are no actual contingency plans in the RAF for dealing with UFOs,' says Jed. 'But the people I talked to were pretty open about them and admitted they didn't know what they were. My suggestion to them was that they would deal with an invasion of air space by an alien craft in exactly the same way as they might have shot down a Soviet Air Force jet over the North Sea during the Cold War. No one disagreed with that and it became the premise from which I worked.'

Jed readily accepts that he did not really expect the RAF to admit to having any contingency plans for UFOs. It was certainly not something that came into his own training and he does not think the topic is very high on the service's agenda. But ...

'One of the guys at the Ministry of Defence I talked to was quite open about the fact he knew pilots who had claimed to have seen unexplained things in the air. Of course, a few years ago that kind of thing would probably have been difficult to talk about. But people are much more open now — especially since the publication of *Open Skies, Closed Minds* by Nick Pope who worked for the Ministry of Defence on their "UFO Desk". He certainly had a much higher security clearance than I ever did, and he insists there is no cover-up going on. Just a lack of understanding what these UFOs might be.'

Jed certainly never intended to use *Invasion: Earth* to suggest that the RAF is keeping anything under wraps.

'In the story, the RAF don't know they have shot down a UFO. They keep referring to a "foreign aircraft", a "breach of airspace" and that sort of thing which grounds the whole thing in credibility. It's only when events begin to unfold that they start to realise that they are dealing with something very different to an earthly foreign power.'

Right from the outset, the production team were determined that 'credibility' would be a by-word during filming of all the flying sequences. They were anxious that viewers would find everything to do with the RAF and the military in *Invasion: Earth* totally convincing. They were not interested in using library shots of jet aircraft or stock footage of RAF bases which can be found in profusion in the BBC archives. Instead they used computer-generated graphics of fighters in the air and the real thing on the ground.

Much of the flying in *Invasion: Earth* occurs over Scotland, in particular in the airspace around Aberdeen where a dramatic confrontation out to sea between a Tornado F3 and a UFO gets the story off to a grab-your-seats start. So the bases to be used for the filming had to be selected with care. After a great deal of location research and negotiation, it was decided to use two of the nation's top bases: RAF Lossiemouth on the Moray Firth, and RAF Leuchars not far from Dundee. Initially, Jed

Mercurio wanted to use RAF Leuchars as the name for his base, but bowed to the service's request to use a Squadron designation instead. Interestingly, the production team opted against RAF West Freugh at Stranraer which actually has a history of UFO reports from 1957 to as recently as 1980. (See 'Close Encounters For the RAF'.)

RAF Lossiemouth is close to the fishing town of the same name located at the most northerly tip of land on the Moray Firth. A rather grey and drab spot, it bears the utilitarian stamp of somewhere that expanded in a hurry to cope with a boom industry – in this case, the nineteenth century herring rush. Yet in the summer months the magnificent stretch of beach transforms the area into a popular holiday resort which attracts tourists from all over the country – especially to visit the harbour where seine-netters go out on the tide and the Lossiemouth Fisheries and Community Museum, which has a reconstruction of Ramsey Madonald's study, the local man who went on to become Prime Minister of Britain.

The RAF base is legendary for its air-sea rescues, and it was here that the production team went to shoot part of the dramatic rescue of Flight Lieutenant Drake after he had shot down a UFO at the beginning of the story and then crashed into the sea himself. But not for the only time on the shoot, things did not work out as planned, Jed remembers somewhat ruefully.

'We wanted to film this search and rescue Sea King helicopter in operation and got everything lined up,' he says. 'The film crew and actors were in place and we just needed the helicopter. Unfortunately at that moment a man on a mountainside had a heart attack and the chopper had to be diverted to rescue the guy. Obviously the RAF considered this far more important than working for the BBC! But because time is money when you have a lot of people on location, we just went ahead and shot the scene – without the helicopter!

'A couple of weeks later we sent a Second Unit back to Lossiemouth and filmed the helicopter on its own. Later we matted this footage with the action scenes we'd got earlier and created a combined shot. Of course, that's just the sort of thing that can happen on location with a story of this kind, but with a little bit of ingenuity everything eventually worked out fine.'

Director Patrick Lau with script supervisor Maggie Lewty and sound man Chandler with Chinook helicopter at RAF Odiham

invasion: earth

There were also problems for the production team to cope with at RAF Leuchars. The base stands on the attractive estuary of Eden and is served by a train platform which is said to be the windiest in Scotland – hardly the most inviting spot! The thunder of the jets taking off also comes up through the soles of the feet and rattles the teeth. Only the aircrew in their bright overalls go purposefully about their assignments as if nothing untoward was happening.

Located on the opposite bank of the Firth of Tay to Dundee, Leuchars is not far from the historic town of St Andrews, perhaps most famous for its Royal and Ancient Golf Club, the ruling body of the sport. The village itself beside the ultra-modern air base is a place where it is not difficult to imagine great moments of Scottish history occurring, especially at the church of St Athernase, one of the loveliest parish churches in Scotland. It was built at the beginning of the thirteenth century by a crusader, Saier de Quinci, and much of the exterior, the arches, and arcades remain exactly as the masons left them. The interior is carved with crusaders' crosses and a series of grotesque heads that might almost be aliens, although they are more likely to represent the crusaders' enemies in the Holy Wars!

The crew and actors from *Invasion: Earth* did their best to avoid being regarded as invaders when they moved into the huge RAF base. Here aircraft take off and land over the great stretch of beach, sand dunes and pine forest known as Tents Muir, and, most appropriately, the station is approached from the south by a little community named Guard Bridge.

'Obviously, the RAF personnel at Leuchars had to carry on with their normal daily activities, and we had to work round them,' Jed recalls. 'The thing was they gave us this guy to smooth our path and he was useless. We had a lot of scenes to shoot of planes taking off and arriving, work going on in the hangers and that sort of thing, so co-operation and co-ordination was essential. But bits of equipment we were expecting didn't arrive on time, and then we'd learn that an aircraft which was supposed to be taking off had taken off earlier!

'Fortunately, our project officer Bernard Grant got into the action and all of a sudden everything started happening. It was still a tricky time for us, though, filming the Tornados in the hangers and then out on the runways and taking off. We wanted to get as much on film as possible. Sometimes in those sort of situations when things

'You can never have enough helicopters . . .'

invasion: earth

don't arrive on time you have to play it off the cuff. You're expecting four missiles and you only get two. You want to use a helicopter for a scene in which a senior RAF officer is supposed to arrive and you can't get one. So you end up shooting the man arriving in a big old Hercules instead. There is always this danger of falling behind on the schedule, so it's either improvise or cut. But things worked out pretty well and we got everything we wanted in the end.'

Jed also took the opportunity during filming at Leuchars to put himself in a scene in the best tradition of director Alfred Hitchcock and author Colin Dexter, the creator of Inspector Morse. It is very much a case of blink-or-you'll miss it, though.

Jed Mercurio: a classic example of Failed Aviator Syndrome!

The scene shows the dispersal of two aircraft to investigate a suspected UFO. One of the Tornados is flown by Flight Lieutenant Drake with his navigator (Stuart McQuarrie) and the other by Squadron Leader Haynes (James Vaughan) with Jed as navigator. Because of his flying experience, it was a procedure the producer enjoyed acting out – and one with which, of course, he was more familiar than the other three.

'For the scene, all four of us were kitted out in flying gear and had to run across the tarmac to the Tornados,' Jed recalls. 'The viewers see James and I running to our aircraft and Vincent and Stuart going to theirs. I don't know how many times we did it, but it was a lot more exhausting than a day as a producer! The joke's on me though, because after all that running around, the way the director shot the scene and the way it's been edited means that you can hardly see me – it really is *just* a moment, and I don't expect even my parents to recognise me!'

To further enhance the authenticity of the flying sequences, the art department under Rod Stratfold's guidance built an exact replica of a Tornado cockpit in order to show the pilots in action in the air. This was erected at Bray studios, placed on gimbels, and filmed against a blue screen on to which the sky and clouds were later matted. An RAF adviser was on hand the whole time to ensure that the movement of the cockpit generated by the gimbels matched those of an actual Tornado in flight, especially the rolling, pitching and banking.

Even working in the studios was not without its hitches, however. The start of filming was delayed when the wrong oxygen masks for the pilots were delivered, which couldn't be fitted to the helmets, and a three-hour delay occurred before the RAF was able to get hold of the correct ones. It was only a detail, but it turned out to be an expensive one because of the cost of hiring Bray and shooting on a blue screen.

Then came a series of discussions between the show's RAF adviser and the director of the first three episodes, Patrick Lau. Patrick is a widely experienced director whose previous credits have included such period series as *The Casebook of Sherlock Holmes* for Granada TV and *Doctor Finlay* for Scottish Television; and *The Fragile Heart* for Channel 4 which Jed particularly admired. The discussions arose during the filming of the cockpit sequences because of the restrictions the technical adviser sometimes wanted to impose on the director's creative eye.

In fact, there were several discussions between the director, the crew and the technical adviser about overcoming the dilemma between telling the story and actually getting to see the characters' faces, and technical accuracy: pilots of these high-velocity aircraft always fly with their masks on and visors down to protect their faces and particularly their eyes in the event of an accident. This is allegedly the same dilemma that faced the director of *Top Gun*: verisimilitude demanded that the actors should have their masks on during the flying sequences, so that's how they were originally shot; but having paid a million dollars for Tom Cruise, the producer was apparently adamant that the audience should get their money's worth and see his face, and insisted that they reshoot!

Jed is full of admiration for the two directors who worked on the series, Patrick Lau and Richard Laxton. Both proved versatile at compensating for anything that went wrong and kept on schedule, though remaining within the budget and not sacrificing the authenticity was, he admits, a constant headache.

Production designer Rod Stratfold in discussion with a member of the Queen's Colour Squadron on location in Scotland

'We had to cut things sometimes,' he says, 'which as producers you know is something you have to do, and still ensure that the story is working. The trouble is you often have to cut those little scenes that just add to the colour of the whole thing. Little gags and things like that end up going. You can write about a hundred gags for a six-hour series like this and about ten of them survive and they're probably not even the really fun ones. They get cut in post-production, and you can just imagine some of the actors seeing that one of their favourite moments has been cut out, and thinking of us, "Oh, they're miserable buggers" – but that's television!'

Close Encounters for the RAF

One of the most famous UFO sightings in Scotland, and certainly the best-known to have been reported by an RAF base, occurred at West Freugh near Luce Bay in Dumfries. The extraordinary events which took place over this rugged and lonely area in April 1957 have been shrouded in mystery until recently when the secret files relating to it were finally declassified.

Reports of unidentified flying objects over this part of Scotland go back to the early fifties. The town of Newton Stewart is nowadays regarded warily as a place where weird magnetic or radio anomalies can happen: all caused by mysterious flying craft. The first of these occurred in October 1955 when what was described as a 'grey, cigar-shaped object with portholes emitting either green or orange light' suddenly flew into the sight of a van being driven out of Newton Stewart towards Luce Bay. As the UFO passed silently over the vehicle and its terrified driver, the engine of the car suddenly stopped.

Since that autumn day, a number of other local residents in the area have reported similar cases of interference to their machinery or radios after sighting objects which, they said, circled over the hills before flying off across the bay. Some have added the information that the UFOs seem to have a red, pulsing light, while one man maintained the craft 'buzzed' as it went overhead.

Two years later it was the turn of a radar operator at RAF West Freugh to add to the mystery. On April 4, the man suddenly noticed an object on his screen which was 'too fast, too big and too manoeuvrable' to be an aircraft. As he watched in amazement, the officer also saw the blip on his screen turn through a number of acute angles beyond the capabilities of any aircraft then known to be flying. The Base Commander, Wing Commander Walter Whitworth, who was summoned to watch the aerial display, also wrote in his report of the events that 'there is no question of the radar playing tricks.'

Such was the impact of the sighting that word eventually got out into the community at large. An official statement was demanded and the lame excuse proferred that the UFO had been a weather balloon launched across the Irish Sea from Northern Ireland! The explanation satisfied no one, but it was not until 1988 when all the documents were released under the thirty year rule for classified information that the balloon story deservedly went up in smoke.

It emerged from the file that several UFOs had been seen in the vicinity of the base at the time – and on previous occasions. All of the craft had been travelling at speeds much faster than any weather balloon could go, and had changed course so frequently that for much of the time they were obviously flying *against* the wind! The balloon story had clearly been a cover-up for something about which the Ministry of Defence could offer no satisfactory explanation.

More proof that RAF West Freugh was being visited by UFOs took place on 12 October 1980. This time an orange oval shape was seen by three Ministry of Defence police officers who were on duty at the base at 3.30 am. The pulsing shape passed across the night sky before flying off towards the sea.

Since that night, the eyes of the men at West Freugh as well as those of the people living around Luce Bay have been regularly trained on the skies waiting for it to return . . .

invasion: earth

the COMING of the ALIENS

Previous page:
The Echo pilot after
crash-landing in
Scotland

The two alien races whose intentions towards the earth are poles apart could not, themselves, be more unalike. On the one hand are the Echoes: peace-loving, humanoid space travellers; on the other the nDs: merciless, organic beings bent on planetary conquest who exist in not just three dimensions, but *four*. In fact, it is the Echoes' obvious affinity with the people of Earth which prompts them to try and warn the planet about the nDs, whose sole objective is to enslave human beings as a commodity and – more terrible still – *a fuel resource*.

The Echo, 1944

It is Nick Shay who first attempts to put a name to the humanoids after he intercepts one of their signals. He suggests Extraterrestrials of Unknown Origin (EUOs), which Flight Lieutenant Drake translates into military phonetic alphabet: Echo Uniform Oscar, soon abbreviated to Echoes.

In truth there is much about the Echoes that is shrouded in mystery. Certainly they are not unlike us in appearance and can breathe oxygen, although they have a lower blood pressure. They are a gentle, rather fragile but highly philosophical and compassionate race who would prefer to lose their own lives than be drawn into violence. They are also very advanced technologically, and capable of interstellar travel within the speed of light.

But where are they *from*? The evidence suggests that their home planet must be a place quite distant from our own solar system. However, because they are limited to slower-than-light travel, it is believed that many of their astronauts may never have seen their home planet, living and working their whole lives in space.

Assuming that the Echo home planet is at least a lifetime away, this would locate it at about two hundred light-years distant. It is obviously a civilised and cultured society built on the foundations of science and morality. The Echoes are not viewed as part of a huge empire, however, but as space-travellers who occupy only a very small area of space and have set up colonies on a number of far-flung planets. The nearest of these to Earth is believed to be about twenty light-years away.

The Echoes use these outposts as the bases for their endless quest, journeying in their highly versatile circular space ships which are identified by the people of Earth as UFOs. These are equipped with escape pods such as the one which crashes on to London at the start of *Invasion: Earth*. The pilots wear tough but very flexible astronaut suits linked by a cable to their air supply. (See 'Costume Design'.)

The extraterrestrials are also equipped with an advanced medical kit that can heal wounds almost instantaneously and a field computer that will locate the user's position anywhere in the galaxy. This remarkable piece of technology can furthermore be used to activate a camouflage system that will make a pilot invisible whenever danger threatens.

As a result of their travels, the Echoes are convinced that intelligent life in the universe is rare and must be preserved. This is what attracts them to the Earth when the first of their spacecraft comes across the great blue planet. Their interest is, though, very much a philanthropic and peaceful one. They have no desire to interfere in the affairs of mankind, merely to warn us against our own follies and the intentions of some other, far deadlier aliens who have also set their sights on the planet with a very different motive.

It becomes clear that the Echoes visited the Earth during the Second World War, that terrible period of modern history when death and destruction went hand in glove with the development of weaponry that would prove the first step towards man himself travelling in space. Today, they are anxious to alert human beings to the still greater danger posed by the nDs, but they are trying to do so in a low-key way in order to avoid creating alarm. The nDs, for their part, know the Echoes are aware of their master-plan, but they have no such reservations about the way in which they will come into contact with the inhabitants of the planet.

At the start of *Invasion: Earth*, the world is caught in the skirmishes between these two advanced alien civilisations. But, in time, the struggle will become focused entirely between man and the nDs: a battle in which a small group of scientists and military men and women hold the key to survival.

The nDs are even more mysterious entities than the Echoes. They are not humanoid in any way, but exist as organic beings in a higher dimension. They are huge in size and their shapes appear to change fluidly. They also possess a power, speed and agility that is truly awesome.

Little is known about the biology of the nDs beyond their obvious need for biological material, which is what attracts them to the teeming planet of Earth. Already, it seems, they have over-run many other worlds without a thought for the indigenous life. Seemingly unstoppable, the nDs take what they need, feed, and make their offspring. But they have no emotions for one another. They don't even seem to *need* each other.

The world from which the nDs comes has an environment almost beyond the imagination of mankind. Possibly based on a planet far off in the galaxy, it is only ever briefly glimpsed. It might just as easily be in a spacecraft or on a way station, and all

Overleaf: The crew filming in 'nD world' at Bray studios

invasion: earth

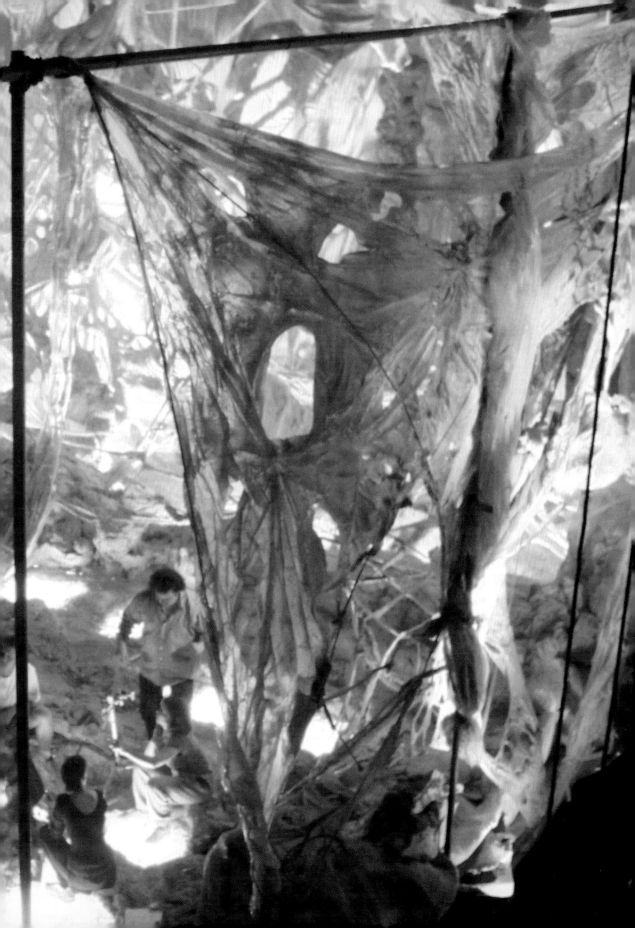

that is certain is that it is here the nDs bring the life-forms upon whom they carry out experimental surgery. It also seems probabley that this world, with its walls like muscles and edges like bone, is actually a mixture of organic and technological matter of a kind humans have never set eyes on before. It is a truly weird and unpleasant place, full of a vast web of fleshy tendrils where the leech-like aliens pursue their inhuman mission. (The nD world created for the series was a major set construction by the art department, led by Rod Stratfold, erected at Bray Studios and later augmented with computer-generated special effects during post-production.)

There can be no doubt that the nDs' science is very far advanced from ours and that of the Echoes. They have developed a means of travelling through the higher dimensions of space in a manner that short-circuits interstellar travel. They do this by way of portals that can distort space and open up channels from one dimension to another. Contemporary physicists sometimes refer to these portals as 'wormholes'. (See 'The nDs' Portals to New Worlds'.)

The nDs' portals appear initially as rays of light bending and circling in the atmosphere. They can be from a few feet high to the size of a mountain and are evidently created by a high-mass source. The crackling sound of this energy building up is followed by straight lines beginning to buckle and curves exaggerating. It is a process that can take some moments to complete and has a blinding effect on those who witness it.

The sight of walls bending is the first and only sign that human beings receive that the nDs are coming. The first, that is, until Nick Shay develops his remarkable detector which resembles a laptop computer and can pick up the energy emissions associated with the nDs' entry into Earth space. Nick says of his invention: 'You might compare it to the invention of radar during World War Two.'

Once in possession of a planet, however, these merciless aliens have a highly efficient system to drain it of all its life-forms, leaving only rocks and non-living structures as mute witnesses to their passing.

It would be easy to think of the nDs as time travellers because of their ability to operate in four dimensions. Indeed, it is a common error to imagine that time *is* the fourth dimension of space after length, width and depth, which, of course, it is not. The fourth dimension can in fact be any dimension at right angles to the other three. The nDs' power to travel in this higher dimension is, to give a simple example, not unlike *our* ability to traverse the air. We are not born with the ability to fly, of course, but we have developed the technology to do so in aircraft.

The aliens can also appear and disappear at will thanks to their special capability of operating in the other dimension. Take, as an illustration of this, the analogy which Dr Amanda Tucker offers during the course of the story. Imagine, she says, living in only two dimensions, in a totally flat land like the floor. Those who dwell in such a place can only appreciate width and length and would not know that depth even existed. Now consider what happens when someone like us – a three-dimensional creature – comes along and passes a hand through this world. At first the only thing the 'flatlander' would see would be five points – the fingertips of the hand. But as the hand passes through, the five points get thicker until, suddenly, when the knuckles have passed by, there is just one big mass. In a world of flat creatures, it might be said, the three-dimensional man would most certainly be king!

It is this mastery of higher space – defined as the 'n Dimension' – which Dr Tucker first experiences when she is taken hostage by the nDs, that enables her to give them their name. Nor do their powers or strangeness end there.

The nDs are, in fact, a pure biotechnology. Their science is based on the manipulation of living tissues, using muscle rather than metal, bones instead of concrete, nerves in place of wires. In fact, all of their machinery is made of living tissue, and they need to gather life-forms from all around the universe to maintain their very existence.

They will kill without compunction and are seemingly able to overcome any obstacles placed in their way. They will also go to any lengths to achieve their objective and no matter what is thrown at them by their intended victims, they invariably find a way to

Dr Amanda Tucker (Maggie O'Neill) imprisoned in nD world

respond. But the nDs *do* have weaknesses. They cannot travel through the portals in large numbers, nor can they live in the Earth's atmosphere for very long. They are completely identical, too – clones of one another – and what can kill one could also kill them all. If there is an antidote to the nDs, it probably lies within the field of biology – perhaps in meeting like with like in biological warfare ...

It does not take the nDs long to realise that the rich biosphere of Earth has much to offer. The planet clearly possesses a complicated chemistry that has developed many different kinds of living things. From these, especially humans, they suspect there is a good deal of raw material that might be extracted for their use. The gaze of the nDs falls on our world like that of inhuman farmers sensing fresh livestock.

The first part of their plan is to poison the Earth's water supplies with oestrogenic compounds in such a way that humanity will believe that pollution is the cause. These compounds of female hormones bring about a fall in the sperm count and it is estimated that by the year 2050, men – whom the nDs regard as the warlike species that must be made docile – will have been replaced by women. But once Earth is an entirely female world, what do the aliens intend next?

SAC Tony Woodward
(Graham Bryan)
held in nD world

The nDs can also seize male and female human guinea-pigs through their portals. Then, using sophisticated surgical techniques, they can imbed cerebral implants into the specimens which may later be activated to start a sequence of programmed behaviour stored in the subconscious. All of these implants will self-destruct if tampered with, causing non-reversible injury. The only option for a carrier is euthanasia.

However, it seems that what *really* interests the nDs about the make-up of human beings is the central nervous system. It is more sophisticated than any other they have found, and undoubtedly contains elements that could be invaluable to

them. On learning precisely *which* of these would further their existence, a primary objective for their invasion becomes abundantly clear.

For the nDs discover the power of a neurotransmitter known to us as serotonin. This mood chemical in the brain which can be acted upon by anti-depressant drugs is equally of interest to today's scientists, because its levels can be effected by 'recreational' drugs like Ecstasy. Furthermore, scientists in America have recently suggested that the reason why even the most ardent male lover has to pause between bouts of passion is because serotonin appears to control the gap between orgasms. It is thought that this discovery could help to produce anti-depressants that do not suppress enjoyment of sex in the way some current prescription drugs do by slowing down the reabsorption of serotonin after it has been released from nerve cells. There is now a possibility that if today's drug designers could create compounds that avoided affecting serotonin in only the critical area – in the case of humans, the region just behind the eyes – they might be able to produce anti-depressants with no effects on sexual function.

However, sexual drive is not the reason why the nDs are so interested in serotonin. They want it for quite a different kind of drive – their own machines. Because the nDs use living tissues in their biotechnology, it is not hard to imagine that all their computers are like living brains – networks of nervous tissues – and the way these nerve tissues send signals is through chemical and electrical transmissions. A vast network of such machinery – which the nDs undoubtedly maintain in their world – obviously requires particular chemicals to run it. Which is where serotonin comes into the formula. The aliens intend to filter it off from humans in much the same way that waste products in the bloodstream are removed by kidney dialysis.

Unknown to the nDs, however, there is a disease associated with serotonin that has the most graphic side-effects. This is known as carcinoid syndrome and it has nothing to do with the brain – it is a tumour which occurs in the intestine and secretes high levels of serotonin into the bloodstream. The effects of the disease are distinct from the mood-altering action of serotonin and result in a very unpleasant physical change in those unfortunate enough to be sufferers. The symptoms include racing heart, flushing, and diarrhoea. Furthermore, for the body to produce large amounts of serotonin, it must use up other chemical stores. Depletion of these (specifically, tryptophan) causes pellagra, which is characterised by scaling and ulceration of the skin. So when the aliens commence their plan with human guinea-pigs, victims succumb to terrible skin damage. The threat of the nDs is, in fact, twofold. They represent not only an invading force, but the they bring a deadly plague, the like of which has not been seen since the days of the Black Death . . .

Costume Design

The space suits worn by the Echoes and Charles Terrell were created for the series by costume designer Howard Burden, whose skill has already been acclaimed in sf circles for his work on *Red Dwarf*, the BBC's long-running cult space opera about life aboard a five-mile long mining ship after a radiation leak.

'Obviously because *Red Dwarf* is a comedy I can do a lot of outrageous things,' explains Howard. 'But the big challenge on *Invasion: Earth* was to create a humanoid, space-suited alien who looks *real*. If it doesn't look real, then I've failed. Now that I've seen the suit in action I *do* believe it works.'

Howard drew on all his experience as a television costume designer along with his extensive research into science fiction on the screen, to come up with the multi-purpose suit which the aliens and Terrell wear to survive in the hostile environment of Earth.

Terrell (Anton Lesser) with the Army doctor (Chris Matthews) attending to the injured Echo pilot, 1944

'In the script we had so many things to cover,' he says with a wry smile. 'Apart from being able to manoeuvre around the escape pod, the alien has to survive in water, scramble up rocks, and run away from his pursuers. So I basically set out to design something that would give the actor maximum mobility to move around and stretch without ripping anything.

'The suit was designed so that there was a membrane skin that sits on top of an infrastructure underneath which shows all the sinews and muscles below. I used stretch polyvinyl, which has a two-way stretch, because it is very durable and has a lot of give in it. It is also so thin that it stretches over the body and this gives it an added texture.'

The suit is completed with several fibreglass panels, a breastplate and helmet which is mirrored so that the viewer catches glimpses of the alien through the visor. Howard is particularly pleased with the finished effect.

'The whole suit gives off light,' he continues. 'It has a really good quality about it. You can almost get a sense of reflection from it without giving too much away. We wanted it to look as interesting as possible without lots of technical gizmos, without lots of lights and trickery. If you send someone into space, he obviously has to have certain monitors and things in order to survive. But because they are aliens of a far greater intelligence than us, they have obviously surpassed anything we could do. I believe the finished look of the space suit achieves this effect.'

From the far future, Howard Burden had to travel back to the past to create the uniforms for the episodes of the story which take place during the Second World War.

'Those wartime uniforms took us a lot of research,' Howard remembers. 'For the modern-day stuff we had the RAF to call on and also a book which gave us the guidelines to the rankings which was fine. Although I have to admit we did allow some variations because as each actor developed his or her personality within a uniform they came up with ideas for slight changes or the way in which they wore the suits. But we still checked everything with the RAF to make sure it was plausible. As a result, I reckon I have learned just about everything to do with what each particular officer would wear in a given situation.

'But for the wartime uniforms we needed to go to the libraries. We wanted to know everything about them, right down to the texture of the cloth. The most interesting thing we discovered was that the fabric then was much coarser – even for civilian clothing. So we got hold of a lot of original 1940s stuff and used this to get a feel of the period. We followed this through when making the uniforms. When they were finished, they did feel a bit like sandpaper. In fact, they were really very uncomfortable and I remember one of the actors saying to me during filming, "My God, did they really wear this stuff and win the war!" '

The nDs' Portals to New Worlds

The nDs' portals through which they enter and leave the Earth with their victims were created entirely with special effects in *Invasion: Earth*. Varying in size from little more than the height of a human being to a gigantic 5,500 feet by 4,500 feet across when the conquest of Earth is launched, these remarkable SFX were all computer-generated by the series' special effects designer, Dennis Lowe, working with one of the leading companies in this area of film production, The Moving Picture Company.

Dennis Lowe is widely regarded as one of the most innovative men in his field with a reputation for using his comparatively small computer system to create the most vast and stunning imagery. Examples of Dennis Lowe's work prior to *Invasion: Earth* can be seen in just two of the pictures he worked on: *Frankenstein* and *The English Patient* (which at first glance would hardly be recognised as an effects-laden movie, but actually needed the work of digital artists on several scenes, including an invasion viewed in flashback featuring fireballs, explosions and parachuting human figures).

For this series, Dennis has used his skill to create among other things the spectacular Tornado fighter crash, the exploding Echo spaceship, and the blinding, shimmering portals of the nDs. After filming the abduction of the victims against a blue screen, the special effects team took over to create the appearance of objects all around them appearing to bend while their bodies folded away into invisibility.

This particular element of the story is made even more fascinating by the fact that the portals are based on a well-known scientific theoretical phenomenon known as a wormhole. It was a decision of the *Invasion: Earth* production team to refer to these structures through space-time as portals rather than wormholes, though both describe a means whereby, one day, interstellar astronauts may be able to jump through hyperspace with much greater ease than by travelling in a spaceship. And certainly a great deal faster.

Maggie O'Neill being assisted by stunt co-ordinator Nick Powell in preparation for blue screen shot

invasion: earth

67

For years, the idea was dismissed as being pure fantasy, although it did have some powerful champions among the leading writers of science fiction. Today, theoretical research in both Britain and America has made considerable progress, adding extensively to the work of the physicists Michael Morris and Kip Thorne who published their benchmark paper on wormholes in 1989.

The concept of wormholes actually began with Einstein's general theory of relativity which states that space-time has a solid structure. In other words, planets, stars and other massive objects create the space and time around them. As the respected physicist John A. Wheeler (the man who coined the term 'black hole' in 1969) has explained further, 'Space is like an ocean which looks flat to the aviator who flies above it – but is a tossing turmoil to the hapless butterfly who falls upon it.'

Drake and Nick Shay run towards the 'phenomenon'

According to Einstein, this entire structure is dotted with wormholes, although their diameter is so small that an atom would appear as large as a planet in comparison. They are so small, in fact, as to be almost impossible to measure. Yet as Einstein's law forbids travel at speeds faster than light, these wormholes might just provide a way of exploring the far reaches of the universe, *if* a way could be found to use them.

Modern physicists have come up with three possible ways of achieving hyperspace travel. The first would be to reduce a space ship and its crew to the size of a wormhole for the journey and then return them to normal size at the other end. But the idea of miniaturisation as a way through tiny wormholes would seem to be impossible.

The second idea has similar drawbacks. This proposes *enlarging* the wormhole by some form of repulsive gravity instead of attractive gravity, so that a normal-sized space machine could travel through it. Again the feasability of such a proposal seems very unlikely.

The third idea, however, has decided possibilities: it suggests searching for large wormholes that may already exist. This theory is based on the belief that when the universe was created 15 billion years ago by the Big Bang, it was infinitesimal in size. The cosmos then achieved the vastness which we know today by repulsive gravity which occurred within a few fractions of a second and inflated everything within it.

nD successfully lured into the trap

Michael Morris, who remains at the forefront of American researchers in the field of hyperspace travel, thinks that this huge inflation might also have enlarged primordial wormholes from sub-microscopic size to diameters of thousands of miles. To find if they exist, he says, it will be necessary for astronomers to monitor thousands of stars to see if their light fluctuates in a particularly unusual way, thereby disclosing the existence of a wormhole. Morris explains, 'I believe that a wormhole that passes between a star and the Earth would force the light of the star behind it to emit twin spikes of light with a dimness in the middle.'

Locating one of these portals would not be the complete answer to hyperspace travel, as each wormhole is believed to divide and sub-divide in such a way that journeying through one could be a navigator's nightmare. In fact, with our present knowledge, there would be no way of being sure where the travellers taking this route might emerge – or even *when*.

The publication in 1988 of Stephen W. Hawking's phenomenally successful *A Brief History of Time: From the Big Bang to Black Holes* has also increased public interest in wormholes. As, furthermore, did the Professor's surprising retraction in October 1995 of his earlier conviction that time travel would never be a practical proposition. 'If you combine Einstein's general theory of relativity with quantum theory, time travel does begin to seem a possibility,' he said.

Continued debate on the subject of wormholes has raised the possibility that they might, in fact, be two black holes linked together by a funnel. Black holes are, of course, stars of sufficient mass which have collapsed and are centred on a singularity (a point where infinite gravity crushes matter and energy completely out of existence) and bounded by an event horizon (defined as the distance from the singularity at which the escape velocity is that of light). The phrase *event horizon* derives from the fact that it is impossible to observe from outside any events occurring closer to the singularity than this.

No matter, though, whether they are referred to as wormholes or portals, the means of interstellar transport used by the nDs in *Invasion: Earth* is undoubtedly beginning to move beyond science fiction to science fact in contemporary mathematics and physics.

Overleaf: nD argues with the word 'successfully' in the previous photograph caption!

the KIRKHAVEN
Phenomenon

Because the UFO sightings around Bonnybridge were so instrumental in the creation of *Invasion: Earth*, the town might have seemed the natural place in which to locate and film the story. In fact, the production team opted to go further north in their search for somewhere more isolated which fitted the demands of the plot. There, about ten miles outside Perth, they came upon Dunning, a town situated at the northern extremity of the Ochil hills. It features prominently in the second half of the series as Kirkhaven, the place marked by the nDs as the focal point for their invasion.

At first glance, Dunning is the 'unremarkable small town' described in the script. Deep in the mountainous heart of the Scottish countryside, it is remote and its brown-stone buildings and houses are rather bleak in appearance. One local guidebook says of it, 'Dunning must be one of those places, in Central Scotland, most frequently signposted and infrequently visited.' Yet in the course of the story it is, in the words of Major General David Reece, destined to become 'the battlefield of the biggest war in history.'

Prior to the invasion, the nDs have pin-pointed twenty-two sites around the world as their groundstations for attack. Kirkhaven, at the time of the story, is the only one active. If the nDs' plan succeeds here, the other twenty-one, including two more in Great Britain, will form a global network of conquest. Unsuspected, the aliens have also been monitoring their human guinea-pigs in Kirkhaven to discover what, if any, medical antidotes exist to thwart their plans.

Major General
Reece (Fred Ward)
with Rapier missile
system at Kirkhaven

It is evident, too, that the nDs have been carrying out their experiments on the people of the little Scottish town for several decades – a fact which is underlined by the discovery that at the last census the village had ten women for every seven men. The first signs of the oncoming crisis occur with the outbreak of an illness that the local GP diagnoses as food poisoning. But when the number of victims starts to grow towards epidemic proportions, panic sets in and despite the best efforts of the local police force, the people of Kirkhaven start to pack up their belongings in vehicles and desert the town – not knowing from what they are fleeing . . .

Chrissy Skinns explains the criteria for selecting Dunning as Kirkhaven. 'We needed a small town that looked typically Scottish and that was also manageable in terms of all the things we had to do to shoot the episodes set there. Going on location is always tough for any television production, but getting the right place to work in can be even harder. All things considered, Dunning worked out pretty well for us. The local people were terribly helpful, and the tower on Dunning's church became a kind of icon in the series: it was so instantly recognisable that we could use it as an establishing shot. As soon as you see it, you know you're in Kirkhaven.'

The logistics of filming any story in a public place are complex enough, but when the plot concerns an alien invasion, an outbreak of disease and a vast portal which threatens to swallow the town and everyone in it, the planning is even more critical. Fortunately, the production team were blessed with good weather for much of their stay in Scotland during the autumn of 1997. The 70-strong crew of actors, actresses and technical staff got on well with the community of Dunning and a number stayed in small hotels or bed and breakfast accommodation forging closer links with the people. It was an invasion by TV the like of which the town had never seen before.

The RAF arrives at Kirkhaven in force

Because of Dunning's position at the hub of three small and unhurried roads with the signs all around indicating the way to the town, a number of local people have begun to wonder if after all the years of isolation their community might become something of a tourist attraction because of *Invasion: Earth*. Could they perhaps become as well-known to tourists as Horsell in England, or even Grovers Mill in New Jersey, USA – the setting for an American dramatisation of H. G. Wells' *The War of the Worlds* in 1938 which generated real-live panic among its audience! (See 'The Panic Broadcast'.)

The town of Dunning has a history which stretches back many centuries as the saddle-back tower of the kirk of St Serf, or Servanus, built in the twelfth century bears eloquent witness. There is evidence of a Roman road running nearby and a bank and ditch in Kincladie Wood which may be a fragment of a Roman camp.

Interestingly, in the light of the filming which took place there, Dunning has survived two earlier invasions. Pictish raiders once tried to over-run the whole moorland region, and later a religious sect known as the 'Culdees', a latter-day off-shoot of the old Celtic missionaries, attempted to evangelise the area. Both were unsuccessful.

Despite its remote location in Stratherne, Dunning has been a flourishing parish for the last two hundred years as the *Gazeteer of Scotland* for 1806 testifies. Then it had a population of 1,504 and consisted of 'a considerable number of houses, many of which have been lately built, are elegant and commodious, and exhibit specimens of architectural taste not often to be met with in a country village.' The same work also makes reference to an adjoining settlement to the south-east referred to as New Pitcairn or, more sinisterly, 'Dragon's Den', which is not to be found on recent maps.

The reason for the houses being 'lately built' is not difficult to discover, and once again is curiously significant in the context of *Invasion: Earth*. Dunning was burned to the ground in 1715 by the Earl of Mar after the Jacobite defeat at Sheriffmuir. Only one house and the church avoided destruction. According to a local legend the sole surviving property belonged to a canny miller who, seeing what was happening, set fire to some damp straw in his kitchen and fooled the arsonists into thinking that their work was as well in hand there as everywhere else! The district also has one claim to literary fame as the birthplace of the poet, Caroline Oliphant (1766–1845), a member of the family who acquired land from Robert the Bruce.

All in all, the town and surrounding district give an excellent impression of a typical Scottish country burgh, and this also impressed Jed Mercurio when he first visited the proposed location.

'The countryside round there is so remote,' he says, 'it has the same kind of isolation you see in American sf movies which are set in the south-western states, usually in desert areas. If you think of the British Isles, some of the most remote, most eerie-looking countryside is in Scotland. So what we found there worked well in terms of narrative and the look we wanted for the location filming.'

At the heart of Dunning lies the church of St Serf and in front of it, Tron Square with what appears to be the shaft of a market cross built into a wall. There are several municipal buildings and offices here which provided the background for scenes in *Invasion: Earth*. On the outskirts of the town lies the Park which commemorates the town's links with the Rollo family who were given the estate by David, Earl of Stratherne in 1380. An inscribed stone bearing the Rollo crest describes how this piece of open land was presented to the parish by John, 12th Lord Rollo, in 1946 to commemorate over 550 years of friendship between the families of Dunning and Duncrub.

Not far from the town stands Keltie Castle, a sixteenth century laird's house, 'long famed for the genuine hospitality of its open and generous-hearted owners', according to the *Gazeteer of Scotland*. This sturdy and attractive building possesses a most unusual defensive structure to beat off any attack – an angle-turret corbelled out above the first floor level which has no fewer than five shot-holes. Near the gateway to the house, there is a cairn standing at the roadside bearing the name Maggie Wall. This unfortunate young girl was burned here as a witch in 1657, but in an act of contrition, local ladies of the parish have ever since taken it in turns to whiten-in the lettering whenever it fades.

The surrounding countryside of Dunning/Kirkhaven on which the nDs focus the portal also has a fascinating history. To the south lies Dunning Common, rising a thousand feet high from the side of a deep dell. About halfway up on what is known as the Black Hill of Kippen stands the Gray Stone, referred to locally as 'The Old Man' – an oddly-shaped, isolated monument, with a commanding view of the local scenery. To the east runs the curiously-named estate of Ha' Towers, now a grass-covered ruin; while to the west is the winding road that leads up into the remote, hidden Ochil valleys of Condie and Struie. This road rises from 160 to 823 feet in a mile and once on the high ground continues pleasantly downwards through a series of hairpin bends to the little hamlet of Path Struie.

The production team made the best of this spectacular scenery both for establishing shots and some of the more dramatic moments in the story. Sometimes they went further afield for particular incidents. The crash-landing of the first Echo escape pod was filmed at Aviemore, for example. The second was shot at Loch Ness – and not without incident! (See 'The Monster of the Loch'.)

The area surrounding Loch Tay was also used for a dramatic episode which Jed Mercurio remembers for two quite different reasons. 'The weather is obviously very important when you are on location – and we only had a couple of really bad days,' he recalls. 'On one of them at Loch Tay we kept filming even though it was pissing with rain. It was so windy, too, that the rain was almost horizontal. We were filming a scene with Wing Commander Friday (Christopher Fairbank) who is one of the victims of the nDs. He is wandering about in the last stages of illness and comes across the reservoir at Kirkhaven.

'Although the rain was falling down we got everyone there and just had to do the scene. Christopher had to go and stand on top of a bridge and look as if he was about to dive in. Of course, a stunt man would do the actual dive, but he still had to do the first bit, tied up there with a safety rope. Christopher did the scene in the wind and rain and I thought it was a really gutsy thing to do, because there is normally no creature that whinges more than an actor. I'm buggered if I would have gone up there!'

Jed made himself useful during the shoot. 'A protective polythene bag suddenly blew off the camera and flew up the cliff side. Obviously the only person on the set with nothing to do is the producer, so I ran up the cliff side to try and get it back. I eventually caught the bag when it got snagged at the top – but nobody noticed or cared! All in all that was a really tough day. There was no real need for me to be there, apart from the fact the crew were getting pissed on with rain and I had to be there getting wet, too. To show you can take it!'

Local schoolchildren stop to watch filming in Dunning

Life was a lot more pleasant for the cast and crew of *Invasion: Earth* while they were filming in Dunning. A number of local houses and buildings were used as exteriors for scenes involving the Kirkhaven Police Station, Doctor's Surgery, and several private homes (the interiors were all built at Caterham). A number of local people were involved as extras, especially for the scenes where the inhabitants of Kirkhaven are seen abandoning their homes, and the filming always attracted onlookers. When word of the shoot spread, the local press ran a story and photographs about the 'New Invasion of Dunning'.

In the main, however, because of the strong military aspects of the events at this juncture in the story, the extras were mostly serving men from The Queen's Colour Squadron of the RAF Regiment. The men came in a convoy equipped with Rapier missiles and military transport of all kinds to add authenticity to the scenes of emergency in the town when the authorities throw up road blocks and seal off the area.

Drake (Vincent Regan) at Kirkhaven

After shooting was over for the day, the crew, actors and RAF personnel often mixed with the people in the nearby towns. In the pubs there was a fair bit of horseplay and noise, but no incidents. But fun was invariably followed by hard work the next day.

The military observation post set up on the outskirts of Kirkhaven echoed to the sound of gunfire and the movement of scurrying troops for several days while the climactic scenes of the nD attack were being filmed. The high drama of these episodes in which controlled explosives and rapid fire weapons were used contrasted sharply with the general high spirits of the crew and the far from infrequent practical jokes of certain actors.

Vincent Regan, who was at the heart of several of these pranks speaks for everyone when he says, 'It was like *Boy's Own* stuff. Every kid who has ever wanted to play at soldiers would have enjoyed the battle scenes at Dunning, popping away at imaginary aliens. While we were busy reacting to something that wasn't there, I couldn't help thinking of that old phrase "the invisible enemy". Ours certainly was!'

invasion: earth

The Panic Broadcast

*'Ladies and gentlemen, I have a grave announcement to make. Incredible
as it may seem, both the observations of science and the evidence of our own
eyes lead to the inescapable assumption that the vanguard of an invading
army from the planet Mars has landed.'*

On the night of Hallowe'en, 31 October 1938, a radio dramatisation in America
of H. G. Wells' *The War of the Worlds* relocated to the rural neighbourhood of
Grovers Mill in New Jersey spectacularly fulfilled its author's desire of creating a
story that was 'within the bounds of possibility'. It came across so realistically that
it seriously frightened a million American listeners and caused several thousand
more who were genuinely terrified to flee their homes in panic. The production had
been masterminded by a 23-year-old radio producer named Orson Welles who, in
fact, went even further than his namesake to authenticate the narrative because he
was afraid the show 'might bore people'.

Despite the fact the broadcast was prefaced with remarks that the events which
followed were fictitious, so well was the dramatic report of an alien invasion of New
Jersey presented (interspersed with breaks for weather forecasts and dance music)
that it created a phenomenon almost unique in the history of communications. Even
the concluding remark of the announcer that it had all been a Hallowe'en prank –
'a radio version of dressing up in a sheet and saying, "Boo!" ' – could not prevent the
growth of a legendary piece of Americana and one of *the* events of social psychology.

Welles chose to move the story to Grovers Mill, a little town of under a
thousand people some fifty miles from New York, for much the same reason the
author had originally chosen Horsell Common. It was a small farming community
of easily recognisable people into whose midst plunged the Martians with their
death rays.

The impact of the actual broadcast was enormously enhanced by Orson Welles'
own performance as the narrator. His magnificent, malleable bass voice, coupled
with his desire to improvise and take with the medium were as impressive as the
outstanding sound effects, each one of which was created with precision and
restraint. From the soft, sinister clawing sound of the Martians when they land, to the
noise of whistling telephone lines and the voices of reporters cut off in mid-sentence,
the radio production moved so effortlessly from grim forboding to straw-clutching
optimism that only the poorest imagination could have failed to be enthralled.

But unease among listeners quickly turned to panic, fuelled, it is now believed, by three other psychological factors. Firstly, with television not yet established, radio was the most vivid medium of communication, and in 1938 audiences trusted it and its news bulletins. Secondly, reports by radio reporters of Hitler's annexation of Austria were still fresh in the memory and the word 'invasion' had become not only one to fear but even seemed a real possibility. Finally, there was the fascination with the idea of Mars being inhabited which scientists and science fiction writers were then both promoting.

A poll conducted shortly afterwards estimated that of the show's six million listeners, more than a quarter were taken in by the broadcast. The front page stories of the nation's press the following morning called the event 'The Night America Panicked' and stories from all over the country told how many people believed the end of the world was at hand. In Boston a woman claimed she could actually 'see the fire' caused by the aliens and she and her neighbours were 'getting out', while in Riverside, the police reported dozens of phone calls from terrified residents spotting the Martians in their giant machines waiting to take possession of New York. A woman in Indianapolis ran into a church shouting, 'New York has been destroyed – it's the end of the world. I just heard it on the radio.' And in San Francisco, people were said to have come forward offering their services against the invaders. 'My God, we've got to stop this thing,' one man was quoted as saying. 'Where can I volunteer?'

Orson Welles making his notorious 'panic broadcast'

DAILY NEWS, MONDAY, OCT

Fake 'War' On Radio Spreads Panic Over U.S.

By GEORGE DIXON.

A radio dramatization of H. G. Wells' "War of the Worlds"—which thousands of people misunderstood as a news broadcast of a current catastrophe in New Jersey—created almost unbelievable scenes of terror in New York, New Jersey, the South and as far west as San Francisco between 8 and 9 o'clock

There was, of course, actually nothing to stop – but there was a public outcry when the nation began to realise how it had been hoodwinked. The papers, which had initially been happy to increase their circulations with sensational accounts of the panic, now turned on Orson Welles. Across the Atlantic, when H. G. Wells heard about the furore he considered taking legal action, although he had given permission for the adaptation. 'I am deeply concerned at the effect of the broadcast,' he cabled from England. 'Totally unwarranted liberties were taken with my book.'

Fortunately, in all the mad scramble to escape the Martians – people taking to the streets; cars racing through traffic lights; and hundreds converging on railway stations – while there *were* numerous injuries, no one was killed. Orson Welles defended himself vigorously, although at the same time encouraging the growth of the legend. When tempers had cooled and rational thinking prevailed, Welles agreed with the theory that *The War of the Worlds* had exploited a mood of fear and radio was the ideal means of doing so. In an interview in 1958 he explained, 'We were fed up with the way everything that came over the magic box was being swallowed. It was an assault on the credibility of that machine.'

The broadcast put Grovers Mill on the map. At a stroke, it turned the little community into a tourist attraction. Sixty years on, Grovers Mill now has a five-foot bronze plaque entitled 'Martian Landing Site' which shows the aliens arriving, Welles at the microphone, and a worried family listening to a radio. This 'memorial to the breadth of man's imagination and the depths of his gullibility', as one paper has described it, inscribed with the words, 'One Million People Believed It', was unveiled on the fiftieth anniversary of the broadcast by the show's scriptwriter, Howard Koch.

Curiously, however, the panic which hit America affected the people of Grovers Mill very little. One resident recalled: 'I heard them say on the radio that the Martians had landed and told my parents. My father said, "Let's go around and see." We asked the police. They didn't know. So we drove around and then went home and didn't think about it any more.'

There was also a remarkable reaction when Radio Braga in northern Portugal broadcast an adaptation of the original play in 1988. This time residents rushed *towards* the spot on the outskirts of the town where the aliens were reportedly landing, although some did flee in cars and the police and fire services were alerted to the alleged Martian invasion by scores of telephone calls. The number of protesters the following day was, though, much more modest than in America – between 150 to 200 people converged on the radio station to complain. There seems no doubt that the grip which a story of alien invasion can exert on the human imagination has lessened very little since Wells wrote his masterpiece a century ago.

The Monster of the Loch

The second escape pod which plunges into a Scottish lake during the present day with an Echo pilot on board provides another of the highlights of the series – one which was demanding on both the film crew and actors. The shooting was not without its curious moments, either.

In the script, the Echo pod is tracked falling to earth on the co-ordinates 55–36–21 north and 01–58–47 west – an unnamed Scottish lake to which Chris Drake, Helen Knox and a retrievals platoon immediately head. To film the splash-down and rescue of the pilot, the production team decided to use the most famous stretch of inland water in the country: Loch Ness.

The dark, peaty-coloured lake near the A82 to Inverness is, of course, said to be the home of an aquatic monster which has been reported since the sixth century and photographed on a number of occasions since the first picture was taken in November 1933 by Hugh Gray. The following April, R. K. Wilson, a Fellow of the Royal College of Surgeons, took what is generally regarded as the classic photograph of a creature with a dark, elephant-grey skin, humped back and long neck. Ever since that day, a great many serious researchers and countless thousands of curious tourists have flocked to Loch Ness in the hope of further sightings and final confirmation that the creature known in popular legend as 'Nessie' actually exists.

Hugh Gray's photograph of Nessie, November 1933

invasion: earth

Far right:
Vincent Regan was
swimming to rescue
the Echo pilot when
something
happened . . .

Below: Echo escape
pod crashed into
Loch Ness

Patrick Lau and the camera crew who went to the lake in late September 1997 were all aware of the story, but no one had any reservations about working on the shore or on the specially-constructed raft to film the sequence of Drake swimming out to the escape pod. The model of the pod was towed out a hundred yards from the shore and moored there prior to being allowed to sink.

For Vincent Regan the swim out to the wood-and-canvas pod was to prove an exhausting – and surprising – experience. He had to run into the lake in full combat gear and swim out to the pod. As it sinks, he is forced to dive under the water to rescue the Echo pilot who has just blown one of the hatches in order to get free. After an agonising wait, both erupt on to the surface with Drake wrenching free the PEC umbilical which still attaches the pilot to the pod.

Vincent is glad he has always been something of a fitness fanatic. 'I enjoy running and swimming, so it was a lot of fun doing the action scenes,' he recalls. 'But that swim in Loch Ness took all my energy. I was just praying Patrick wouldn't make me do it too many times! There was one thing, though, that happened during the shoot which I'll never forget.

'I was in the middle of trying to rescue the alien when I had to dive underwater. I suddenly felt something tug at my leg. I turned round and looked into the water. I then saw a large shape disappearing into the depths. I don't know what it was . . .'

A number of visitors to Loch Ness who came across the crew during filming were momentarily startled into thinking they were actually seeing Nessie as the strangely-shaped pod slid beneath the surface of the water. One visitor to the lake who had been coming for over ten years in the hope of a sighting was disappointed to discover it was only a film crew on location.

A curious legend that a number of photographs taken at Loch Ness have subsequently been jinxed seems to have occurred to Gary Moyes, the location photographer who visited the set on September 23. In the past, a number of photographs of the monster have been accidentally destroyed or lost. The Cornish investigator, Doc Shiels, who took some pictures in 1971 tells the best-known story of this kind:

'My original number one colour slide went astray for days on end at the *Daily Record* offices in Glasgow. Other photographs from the same roll of film vanished entirely. My original number two slide somehow escaped from its carefully sealed envelope somewhere between Cornwall and Boston, Massachusetts. The only direct, negative, monochrome, glass copy-plate made from that slide was accidentally dropped and broken – by me! It's a disturbing fact that hardly any of the original negatives of the better-known Loch Ness monster photographs taken since 1933 have survived. Nessie pictures are supernaturally accident-prone!'

It wasn't a picture of a monster that Gary Moyes took which proved accident-prone, but a straight-forward publicity shot of a dripping Vincent Regan holding the rescued Echo pilot (Nicola Buckingham) in his arms as he steps from the water of the loch. The sun is setting over the mountains behind the couple, forming an ideal backdrop. But a strange shape in the sky to their left immediately catches the eye when the negative is studied.

It shows a disc-shape with what appears to be air turbulence in its wake and bears a weirdly similar appearance to the popular concept of a UFO or Flying Saucer . . . unfortunately, it's just Gary Moyes' finger!

the BATTLE
Personnel

A GUIDE TO
THE SPECIAL TASK FORCE

DRAKE, Christopher

Flight Lieutenant, RAF

[Played by Vincent Regan]

Flight Lieutenant Chris Drake is one of today's front-line RAF fighter pilots. Intelligent, strong-minded and self-centred, he starts out on his mission in *Invasion: Earth* in his own words as 'an arrogant son-of-a-bitch'. But fate, in the shape of an alien shoot-out, a tussle with military bureaucracy, and the arrival in his life of an equally strong-willed woman, Dr Amanda Tucker, brings out the good guy in Drake's nature.

He is a highly-skilled pilot in his early thirties. He has been in the RAF for about eight years and seen a good deal of action in the Gulf War and Bosnia before his encounter with a UFO over the North Sea which ignites the drama in

the series. Vincent Regan says he has found playing Drake 'a really interesting journey' in more ways than one.

'At the start of the story, he is very much from the reckless school of British aviation,' says Vincent. 'He decides what he is going to do in the air and he does it. As a result of that, he shoots down a UFO because he thinks the spacecraft has attacked him. He deliberately disobeys an order not to fire and so he ends up being grounded. And he feels pretty wounded about that because he believes he was just retaliating in the way any airman would do if attacked.

'But once he realises what the threat *really* is, he starts to learn more about himself. He falls in love for the first time, too, and also gains a lesson in humility, especially when he confronts the nDs in the later episodes. He gets knocked back all the time, and for an arrogant man getting knocked back is hard to handle. Discovering love with Amanda Tucker is what gives him the strength to carry on – even when she commits the ultimate sacrifice,' Vincent adds.

Vincent Regan has a lot of charm, a ready wit, and an inclination to reply to questions with tongue in cheek. His family originated in County Rosscommon, although he was born in Swansea, which he reckons still gives him a Celtic heritage. Always determined to be an actor, he began in a number of fringe stage productions for the Moving Theatre Company, The Landor and the West Yorkshire Playhouse before joining the Royal Shakespeare Company.

'I spent three years with them doing all that proper acting stuff with wigs and beards and swords,' recalls Vincent. 'Then I went into TV and I've been on quite a number of popular series including *London's Burning, A Touch of Frost, Peak Practice* and *The Bill.* I've also done some films including *Black Beauty* and *When Animals Attack.*'

Vincent actually came to *Invasion: Earth* with some experience of playing a pilot. He appeared as a helicopter pilot in the series *Call Red*, which, he says, helped him to understand the basics of aviation. But before playing Flight Lieutenant Drake he read a lot of source material on the life of modern combat pilots and spent some time with a group of serving officers at RAF Leuchars.

'It's a fascinating place,' he recalls. 'The RAF are up there to guard the North Sea. Originally it was from the threat of the Russians, but now the Cold War is over they have different duties. I did have an inkling of the way pilots behave from *Call Red* – the posturing and the arrogance. But they are not all necessarily in the Tom Cruise image; a lot of them are very intelligent men. Which, of course, you have to be when you are throwing a £30 million aircraft around the sky at 700 mph! I certainly wouldn't want to crash one and come back holding a parachute and say, "Sorry – that's all I've got left!" '

Vincent is also something of a science fiction fan which was another factor that attracted him to *Invasion: Earth.* 'I've read a lot of sci-fi,' he says, 'and I love watching it on cable and the Sci-Fi Channel. Recently, I've been catching up on the old episodes of *The Twilight Zone.* I'm also pretty clued up on all the conspiracy theories which helped with playing the role, too. Actually, it's all been great fun, and if someone had told me when I was nine or ten that this would be what I was doing when I grew up, I'd have said, "I wish!" '

One of the great pleasures for Vincent in making the series was working with Fred Ward who, he says, has been a hero of his for years. That, and seeing the beautiful wildness of Scotland because parts of it reminded him of Ireland.

'I love being able to get away to Ireland and spend some time with my father there. It is just so peaceful and so different from Brixton which is where I live in London – and that is full on!'

KNOX, Helen

Squadron Leader, RAF

[Played by Phyllis Logan]

Squadron Leader Helen Knox is the very efficient, by-the-book, second-in-command to Major General Reece. She is dedicated to the RAF and good at her job. But becoming involved in an invasion by extraterrestrials is not something she finds easy to accept, as Phyllis Logan who plays the role explains.

'Right up until there is an alien practically in her face, Helen will not countenance that this is anything other than a Russian invasion. She is a bit hidebound by convention, I would say. But when she does come round to everyone else's way of thinking, she goes with it whole-heartedly.'

Helen is a career woman, married to an RAF officer who is on an overseas posting at the time of the events in *Invasion: Earth*. A precise, highly-motivated and attractive red-head, she is as particular with her appearance as she is in her dealings with others. She has no reservations whatsoever about ordering men around.

'That was very nice – it made a real change for me,' recalls Phyllis. 'I thought it was quite sweet that some of the guys reckoned they would have a nickname for Knox – probably Fort. Which I thought was quite amusing. We suggested it to Jed, but it didn't make it into the script. I think that should be her epitaph: Fort.'

For Phyllis Logan, who was born in Paisley, filming in Scotland was a refreshing change as she had not worked in her native country for some years. Trained at the Royal Scottish Academy of Music and Drama, she appeared with a number of small theatre companies in Scotland including the Netherbow Theatre, the Traverse Theatre and at the Edinburgh Festival before entering the world of films and winning both the BAFTA Award for Outstanding Newcomer to Films and the *Evening Standard* award for Best Actress in *Another Time, Another Place* in 1983. Since then she has become a familiar face on television in a variety of leading roles in series such as *Lovejoy* (the unforgettable Lady Jane), *Kavanagh Q.C.*, *An Unsuitable Job for a Woman* and *Inspector Morse*.

Phyllis relished being able to use her natural Scottish accent again and put a lot of research into making Squadron Leader Knox a totally believable figure.

'I was very fortunate in that I got to spend time with a female Squadron Leader in charge of training at RAF Uxbridge,' says Phyllis. 'Basically, she had an office job, which I suppose is what Helen would do if it weren't for the alien invasion. That was very useful, because it enabled me to see the officer in all her guises.

'Not long before, she had actually been in a similar role to mine as an aide-de-camp, working for the man who organised the displays of the Red Arrows. She flew all over the world with him and this meant wearing all kinds of uniforms, flying suits, even combat fatigues. She had photographs of herself in all of these, and she took me through them, showing me how they should be worn, how they should be pressed – all those sort of details which are very important for authenticity.'

Phyllis' contact at RAF Uxbridge was also able to help her round out the character of Squadron Leader Knox.

'She told me she was married to a Flight Lieutenant who had been posted abroad. Although they had a house in Leicester which they had had from the time they'd been posted there, they only met up at weekends when one or other wasn't abroad. It didn't seem to me to make for a stable home life, but apparently the chances of promotion for a woman in the RAF are that much better if you are married. So although there was not a lot about Helen's background in the script, that seemed to me the kind of back-story that would fit her character.

invasion: earth

'It really was very helpful to meet my equivalent in real life. You've got this notion in your head that they are a different breed – which of course they *are* to some extent. But basically they are just like normal, everyday folk getting on with their jobs – which seems to involve office work or hanging about. A bit like being on a film set, I suppose, waiting for something to happen!'

It would be wrong to imagine that Phyllis Logan's work on *Invasion: Earth* was without its incidents, however.

'Guns and explosions aren't usually my bag,' she says with a grin. 'But I had to fire a pistol in one scene. It was shot on the James Bond stage at Pinewood. It was quite scary because I didn't realise I actually had to do it until I came face to face with an armourer. "Can we go outside and practise for a bit?" he asked me. "Practise what?" I said. "Oh, you will be firing your gun in the next scene."

'When we came to film the scene the gun going off was deafening. All the more so because we were on this big sound stage that reverberated like mad. We all had our yellow ear plugs in which were suitably camouflaged by the make-up department. The trouble was we couldn't hear the director shout, "Action!", "Stop!" or anything.'

Squadron Leader Knox also takes part in one of the climactic flying moments of *Invasion: Earth*.

'I didn't actually have to *fly* a plane,' she says. 'I was just sitting on a seat in the studio, strapped in, and pretending I was in a cockpit. I suppose it was a bit unusual – getting buffeted up and down on a platform by the prop guys. I have to admit I can't wait to see how it looks on the screen!'

Phyllis does not consider herself a great fan of science fiction although she did enjoy watching *Lost in Space* and *Star Trek* on television.

'But it was different and very nice to be involved in something like *Invasion: Earth* – especially reacting to aliens. Even though the RAF guys couldn't say exactly how they would react in such a situation, we had to busk it within the confines of how the service operates. You have to keep some semblance of reality whether you think an alien invasion is a possibility or not.

'As far as acting to aliens is concerned, all actors have to do that so many times in their careers. You know, acting to something that is not there – an oncoming lorry, a jet overhead, or, in this case, an alien emerging from a portal to wreak havoc. So you adopt a response: look suitably horrified and hope the audience is, too!'

Group Captain Susan Preston is a multi-skilled officer who is both a neurosurgeon and scientist. As a top woman surgeon, she is probably unique in the military. Although always very focused in her work, there is an underlying scepticism in Susan's nature which comes to the surface when she is asked to perform an operation on a patient believed to be the victim of an alien implant. However, once she is aware of the terrible dangers facing the world, no one works harder than Group Captain Preston to counteract the sickness that threatens to strike down countless victims . . .

'When she is asked by the MoD to operate on this person who has been abducted by aliens and then returned, she is very doubtful about the whole story,' explains Sara Kestelman who plays the Group Captain with great authority. 'You know how medical people and scientists are – it has to be either black or white. There is no room for any grey in between. I think that is very much part of her mode as a person, too, and probably what got her where she is in the top echelons of the RAF.

'What she finds during the operation is very shocking to her and changes her mind completely. She discovers something that has nothing to do with man, nothing to do with people on Earth. It is a problem that must be addressed at once. When other evidence of foreign tissue is produced and then an actual alien is brought to the base for a post-mortem, she is completely on board.'

Sara Kestelman brings the experience of a varied and accomplished career in theatre, film and television to bear on what she describes as 'a very strong woman's part' which she was thrilled to be asked to play. Trained as a dancer and then at the Central School of Speech and Drama, she spent her early years with the Royal Shakespeare Company playing classical drama. Her later work on the stage has included everything from Alan Ayckbourn's *Bedroom Farce* to Golda in *Fiddler on the Roof* and a co-starring role with Maggie Smith and Samantha Bond in *Three Tall Women*. Sara has starred in movies such as Ken Russell's *Lisztomania*, *Zardoz* with Sean Connery and in the role of Frances Grey in *Lady Jane* directed by Trevor Nunn. On television she has been seen in *Bergerac*, *Kavanagh Q.C.*, and as Dr Sophia Blake in the BBC Scotland series, *The Walls of Jericho*. For her performance as Fraulein Schneider in *Cabaret* for Carlton TV she won an Olivier Award for Best Supporting Performance in a Musical.

invasion: earth

Sara happened to be in Scotland when *Invasion: Earth* was being set up and didn't need asking twice to take on the role of Group Captain Preston which, she says, is unlike anything she had played before. She also did more research for the role than any other.

'I felt it was very important because of what the character was asked to do that I should know exactly how it looked and felt,' she says. 'It needed to be like second nature. I have always been terribly squeamish about blood, gore and opening up bodies, and if you had asked me six months ago whether I would watch a brain operation taking place I would have said absolutely no way. But in fact I *did*. I went to the National Hospital of Neurology and Neurosurgery and saw a brain surgeon at work from start to finish – and without fainting!

'I also spoke to some people in the military to find out what it is like to be a medical person in the RAF. I watched a tape of a post-mortem made for students at the University of Glasgow, and got out my family medical book full of illustrations and mugged up on that. I made a lot of notes and even did a few tracings of parts of the human body to help me *be* the part.'

Before filming began, Sara took the opportunity to widen her knowledge of UFOs and aliens. She was particularly intrigued with a television report on the Roswell Incident which included details of the autopsy on one of the alien crew.

'There was also a woman who claimed to have been abducted,' Sara goes on. 'She was absolutely adamant. Afterwards she said she felt something in her foot – something that wasn't quite right. So she went to her doctor and when he examined her he found an implant in her heel. I remember looking at that and thinking, "That's incredible." Because it is *just* what happens in our story, although in a different part of the body. I was just so stunned with the similarity between fact and fiction.'

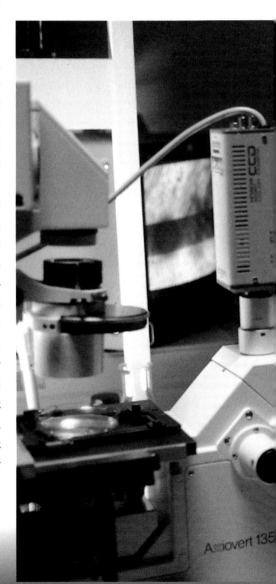

Axiovert 135

On the sets of *Invasion: Earth*, Sara enjoyed working with her assistant, Flight Lieutenant Tim Stewart (Bob Barrett) in the race to discover what has infected people and then developing a toxin to counteract the sickness. Her earlier research proved invaluable when it came to giving verisimilitude to the scenes in the science and medical units where the pair test soil samples, examine tissues and when Susan herself has to perform the delicate brain operation which ends in tragedy, but convinces her of the severity of the situation.

'Despite the high pitch of the story, it was a very calm set with a wonderful crew,' she adds. 'Although the directors Patrick Lau and Richard Laxton have different approaches, they complemented each other and created the kind of atmosphere that is good to work in. To have been asked to play a Group Captain in the RAF would have been a surprising departure for me – but to play one who is also a scientist and a neurosurgeon was an absolute delight!'

invasion: earth

RADCLIFFE, Jim
Flight Lieutenant, RAF Regiment
[Played by Jo Dow]

Flight Lieutenant Jim Radcliffe is a down-to-earth member of the RAF Regiment – the military division of the service – who finds it difficult to come to terms with the idea of an alien invasion. He is in charge of the group of men sent to pick up the crashed pilot of the UFO in Scotland and finds himself confronted with a being who can apparently disappear at will. Yet he still cannot quite believe the evidence of his own eyes, according to Jo Dow who plays the role.

'Radcliffe is almost the antithesis of Flight Lieutenant Drake,' he explains. 'Drake is more of an impulsive loner, because he's used to flying on his own. Radcliffe is always a group man and in charge of people. He responds to things much more logically, so it is difficult for him to come to terms with the idea of alien beings. His imagination doesn't stretch that far, and so it takes him a long time to be persuaded that *this* is something quite different to the normal enemy they are used to fighting. His attitude is to shoot anything that moves and ask questions afterwards.'

Radcliffe is, though, full of admiration for Major General Reece who leads the alien task force, says Jo. 'He probably hero-worships him, I guess, because Reece is every soldier's kind of general. Radcliffe follows his orders to the letter because that is what he is trained to do.'

Invasion: Earth is the second Jed Mercurio project that Jo Dow has worked on, having played the gay medic, Dr James Mortimer, in *Cardiac Arrest*. Six foot tall and darkly handsome, Jonathan Bell Dow was born in Redditch, Worcestershire and trained at the Guildhall School of Music and Drama. His early work was on the stage at the Sherman Theatre as Headboy in *Forty Years On*, followed by *Les Liason Dangereuses* and *Hangover Square* in London. On television he has appeared in *Casualty*, *Dangerfield*, *London's Burning* as well as becoming a familiar face as P. C. Stringer in *The Bill*.

Jo has a mischievous sense of humour and once listed in an A-Z of TV stars that his favourite pet was a spider! He found working with real RAF soldiers during the shooting of *Invasion: Earth* not without its funny side.

'Of course, they think we are all a bunch of pansies when the make-up girls come round and put make-up on our faces,' he smiles. 'But we had a laugh of our own when they appeared with their camouflage make-up before going off into the undergrowth!'

invasion: earth

To learn more about the life of an RAF soldier, Jo spent some time at RAF Uxbridge. 'But there is only so much you can do because you can't expect to catch up on ten years of training and experience in a few days,' he says. 'The one thing I did notice was the casualness of the guys. Playing a ranking officer was what worried me the most. How do you play rank? I wondered how someone could salute a person that they couldn't stand or didn't respect. I was told that you are saluting the colour and the fact that you belong to the same regiment. Other than that the officers are very relaxed and informal or else they would all have to go around saluting each other all the time. Mind you, the one time I did salute, a member of the RAF Regiment rushed over and told me my thumb was in the wrong place!'

Guidance from serving officers was, in fact, very useful to Jo and the other actors – but not always without its problems.

'Their advice was helpful, but sometimes a bit confusing when they wanted everything to be technically correct,' he explains. 'They pride themselves on getting everything looking just right, but in the end as an actor you have to make the scene work. So sometimes we had to say, "Thanks for the technical stuff, but we've got to make it look dramatic." '

Jo is interested in science fiction and has been keeping abreast of the latest reported UFO sightings. He was particularly fascinated by the story of Bonnybridge.

'There has been this massive wave of sci-fi really catching on everywhere,' he says. 'I think it has to do with the Millennium and the end of the century. There is such a change in technology occurring so rapidly. Where can we go but upwards?'

He believes that *Invasion: Earth* has a point to make about man's warlike nature. 'What the two types of alien creatures in the story represent to me is that one is a peaceful power and the other is completely warlike and we are somewhere between the two. What Terrell seems to be telling us is that even if we do take notice of what he says, we will still probably end up killing ourselves because of our nature.'

Jo found filming the confrontation scenes with the nDs at Kirkhaven some of the hardest he has ever had to play.

'You don't know what you are looking at. You can't compare it to the last time you saw an alien. So I was dredging the depths of my "sense memory" as the Americans call it in order to find out how to react to each bit. There was one scene where we were about to let off a nuclear weapon. When did I ever do that? How would that feel?'

Flight Lieutenant Radcliffe is actually on the hillside at Kirkhaven when the nDs launch their invasion of Earth through a portal.

'That was such a weird day of filming,' Jo recalls. 'I actually had to do shot after shot from four different angles. And in each one the portal was getting bigger. So there I was on this hillside in Scotland saying, "Oh!" and then "Oh, it's bigger!" How do you top that over and over again, and still know where you are on your scale? I did chat to the SFX guy to ask him what it was we were looking at so that I could try and get some kind of mental image, but it was extremely hard.'

Jo's sense of humour never deserted him during shooting. He was disappointed not to have filmed at Loch Ness – 'I would have had my head in the water the whole time' – and did consider making up a UFO sighting for a publicity stunt.

'But I didn't take that seriously for long,' he adds. 'The human element of the story, the imagination in it, the predictions for the future and the technology, are all much more fascinating.'

invasion: earth

Major General David Reece is an American Air Force General who has been assigned to NATO. A career airman who has worked his way up in the ranks, he is a man ready to accept responsibility, driven by a strong sense of duty and morality. He has been brought to the screen at the centre of a global crisis with notable gravitas by the American actor, Fred Ward.

'The General is a man who has to be convinced of something before he will take action,' says Fred. 'He has stepped into a massive responsibility, and to start with he wants to do everything through the chain of command, making sure he has permission to go ahead. He is reluctant to take action because he doesn't think anyone in authority will believe the story about aliens.

'I think, basically, he is an American moralist – not in a bad sense – but he has to believe in something before he can do it. He is ready to take the blame if he makes a mistake, sure, but he believes what he is doing is really necessary and important. I think the General also understands the bureaucracy of the military: that if he hands anything over to someone else it may just disappear. For you know, people tend to pass the buck pretty easily in bureaucratic systems.'

For Fred Ward, making *Invasion: Earth* was his first introduction to working for British television, although he is a widely-respected actor who has appeared in innumerable plays, films and television productions in America. Born in California, he has worked in theatres in New York, San Francisco and Rome. His list of movies includes memorable performances in *Escape From Alcatraz* directed by Clint Eastwood, *The Blue Villa* for Alain Robbe-Grillet, *The Player* and *Short Cuts* with Robert Altman and *The Right Stuff* which Philip Kaufman directed. And on US television, Fred has been seen in *First Do No Harm*, *Cast A Deadly Spell* and *Noon Wine*.

The BBC series is not, though, his first brush with science fiction. In 1983 he starred in *Timerider* as Lyle Swann, a motorcyclist who careers into a time travel experiment and finds himself transported back to the old Wild West, where he tangles with the outlaw Peter Coyote and romances Belinda Bauer so that she can turn out to be his own great-grandmother! Though not a big commercial success, the film does prefigure the hugely successful *Back to the Future III* by mixing twentieth century technology with nineteenth century generic conventions.

Fred Ward accepted the role in *Invasion: Earth* on the basis of the early scripts, and for the opportunity it gave him of working with British actors. Although he found the assignment 'like shooting three films in one, the same kind of schedule,' he has no cause to regret his decision.

'I was in the UK from the start of the shoot. London is one of the great cities of the world and I had a fine time there. Scotland, too, was wonderful. The people on location were very kind and generous, especially the locals when we were shooting out of doors. I went up to Glencoe while I was there and that was kind of mythical – beautiful and haunting.'

Fred admits that he didn't spend a lot of time researching the Major General's background, preferring – as he puts it – 'to work on my feet.'

'I just know there is a lot at stake for him because he is a man who has worked his way up. There might even be a little fear of his superiors laughing at him. One little *faux pas* and he is back on the training ground – it could all be taken away from him. Yes, I really enjoyed playing the character.'

Like the other actors, Fred found acting to aliens that they cannot see a big challenge. 'But then all acting in itself is a challenge,' he reflects. 'To believe in what you are doing. As an actor, being on location can be both good and bad. You are jerked out of your own life and thrown in with a group of people you have never met before. On day one, everyone is a stranger, but I was pleased at how quickly we all became co-workers. I was surprised at how similar working here is to the States – the way things are shot and most of the terminology is the same. I was kind of thinking it would be different.'

Fred Ward remains unsure as to whether aliens really exist, but has a theory as to why science fiction has become so popular with the general public.

'I think it is a kind of metaphor for a lot of things. Maybe in the fifties, sf was a metaphor of the Reds-under-the-beds scare. Today, the fear seems to be of a virus that could kill off the world – Ebola, HIV or some bacteria which is immune to antibiotics. Maybe there always has to be a fear in the collective unconscious. Or maybe people just like a good scare story!'

Nick Shay is the brilliant whiz-kid computer scientist whose off-beat looks belie his intelligence and single-minded determination. He believes passionately in the existence of extraterrestrials and his mastery of the computer and knowledge of space has turned his search for intelligent life into almost an obsession. Nick in fact presented a study in contrasts for the versatile actor, Paul J. Medford.

'He doesn't look anything like he acts,' says Paul with a wide grin. 'He looks like a New Age traveller who really should be at Glastonbury rather than in a laboratory or in any kind of place dealing with UFOs. But he has a keen interest in the subject and he has waited for ages for the aliens to come because he believes they are out there. No matter what, they are out there. So when they arrive, his day is made.'

invasion: earth

Nick Shay is actually a very laid-back guy. He has already been around the world and spent three months backpacking in Thailand. It is all this travelling, his friends suggest, that perhaps accounts for his constant hunger which he is forever trying to satisfy with crisps and chocolate! He is worldly-wise, but possesses an interest in the paranormal that is profound and well-informed. But his face and clothes certainly give those who meet him the initial impression that his interests should be anything but higher science and technology.

The role calls for Paul to wear dreadlocks, nose jewellery and earrings, plus a UFO T-shirt and trainers.

'It was great fun wearing all those things,' he says. 'Initially, the hair took a day to get in, and then each day in make-up it had to be made to stand up again. I'm not going to keep the extensions after the shoot, though!'

Paul came to the series with a wide range of theatre and television experience despite his youth. Born in London, he trained at RADA, and made a number of appearances with small theatre companies in productions like *Roll With The Punches* and *Sweeney Todd*. He performed for Michael Bogdanov in *Hair* at the Old Vic, was in Richard Eyre's *The Changeling* at the Royal National Theatre, and received rave notices along with his co-stars in the long-running musical *Five Guys Named Moe*. Paul has been seen on television in *Call Red*, *The Chief* and *Something Wrong in Paradise* in which he played Seenoevil with Kid Creole and The Coconuts, although he is probably best known for his role as Kelvin in the BBC's soap, *EastEnders*. His talent has already been recognised with a nomination for an Olivier award for Best Actor in a Musical, and in 1995 he received the Society of Black Arts Achievement Award.

In *Invasion: Earth*, Nick Shay works closely with Dr Amanda Tucker whom he has known since his university days. Both share the same passion for SETI.

'Dr Tucker is his mentor,' explains Paul. 'She in fact got him through his degree and fired his interest in extraterrestrials. Now they love working together because they actually believe there is something up there. They have been waiting for ages for something to happen – it is their whole lives, really. And then just as Nick is about to bite into another piece of chocolate he notices a glitch in the satellite beam and the whole story takes off. Mind you, his appetite does go somewhat when the aliens actually arrive and it all gets a bit frightening!'

Paul had never appeared in a science fiction production before, but worked hard to master the intricacies of the part of a computer expert.

'There were lots of scientific words I had to learn,' Paul recalls, 'and lots of technical jargon which I had to understand in order to say it convincingly. It was all a bit like going back to school and doing 'A' level Maths. But it was something new for me and all great fun.'

Flight Lieutenant Tim Stewart is the RAF medical officer who finds himself thrust into the race against time to find an antidote to the alien disease. He is both inspired and a little awed at having the chance to work with Group Captain Susan Preston, but the pair get on well together and become well co-ordinated partners. Bob Barrett, who plays the Lieutenant, found the part an interesting one and not without its moments of surprise.

'Once we start working together, Susan Preston and I become more important in the sense that we are the people who tend to the sick and try to find out what is going on,' says Bob with a smile. 'We are in the white heat of what is happening in medical terms, and that provides you with splendid opportunities as an actor. It is just a pity that when we find the antidote it seems too late.'

Playing a doctor with strong scientific inclinations for experimentation was not too much of a problem for Bob Barrett as he has already appeared in *Casualty* as a registrar, and as a scientist in *An Unsuitable Job For A Woman*, both of which, he believes, helped him with the role of Tim Stewart. That – and the research which he put into the part.

'I was lucky in that we had a medical officer on the set right from the word go and he could put me right on all the kind of things someone in my position would do. I also had the chance to see one of the best brain surgeons in the country perform an aneurysm at the Royal Hospital for Neurology and Neurosurgery. It was extraordinary – the kind of thing you dream of.

'When we went there I expected to find a doctor in his fifties, but he was only 32. He had got on the fast track and become one of the leading surgeons in the country very quickly. I could relate to that, because I'm 31 and playing an assistant to someone high-powered like him. He was a great bloke and the person I clung to in terms of research.'

invasion: earth

Bob Barrett's career began at the Guildhall School of Music and Drama in the late eighties. It has, in fact, involved him in a fair amount of research, along the way earning him selection for the prestigious William Poel Festival at the Olivier Theatre. His early stage experience was in the classics such as *Uncle Vanya* (playing Telyeghin), *Hamlet* (Horatio), *A Midsummer Night's Dream* (Demetrius) and powerful modern dramas like *Of Mice and Men*, *Abigail's Party* and *Damned For Despair*.

While researching for *Invasion: Earth*, Bob also spent some time at RAF Uxbridge and sat in the cockpit of a jet. He talked to a number of the personnel at the station, wore combat gear, and generally did everything he hoped would give him a feel for the military side of his role as a Flight Lieutenant.

He is also a great fan of science fiction and was delighted when offered the part in *Invasion: Earth*. He particularly admires the *Quatermass* TV series and the movie, *Alien*, which he believes worked especially well because it has an invisible force that the audience do not see until late on in the story, making it twice as scary and threatening. Bob believes the BBC series will have a similar impact on viewers.

'Stories like this when done from a very human point of view can be fantastic. It isn't so much a story about watching other life-forms, as watching what the events do to the human soul and in particular the RAF people. There is a really tense and dramatic feel about the whole thing.'

Bob himself went through quite a tense and dramatic time during one part of the filming, as he explains. 'I was playing this scene with Sara where we try to resuscitate the Echo. It was an enormous *ER*-type scene with lots of people rushing about and trying to shock the alien back into life. Now just then my wife was expecting a baby – our first child – and I was terrified I wouldn't be at the birth. Patrick Lau was great and he allowed a mobile phone on the set in case anything happened while we were filming. I was shaking all the time, and Fred Ward said later that it was one of the funniest day's filming he had ever done. We got through this incredibly tense scene and then everyone just started cracking up – falling about with laughter. It was ages before we could get back to filming again.

'The baby was not actually born until a week later. By then everybody was dying for it to happen. If it had happened while I was on the set, they were going to bring the mobile to me, turn the camera on, and tell me the baby was being born. I would have flipped out! They had it all planned – they were going to get me on film as I passed out!'

This is not quite the end of the story of Bob Barrett's baby, which the proud parents named Eleanor Rose. 'It was quite extraordinary, because out of the five couples who went to the NCT group with us, all five had girls. After they had been delivered, I thought, "Oh, my God, the script – it's actually happening. No boys *are* being born!" It was a very strange moment and one I'll never forget.'

Lieutenant Charles Terrell is the leader of a bomb disposal unit during the Second World War who inadvertently becomes the spokesman for the Echoes in their attempt to save the Earth from invasion. A cultured man from a privileged background who taught anthropology at Cambridge before the war, he is the kind of officer who breaks the stereotype and is therefore not trusted by his colleagues. Terrell is sensitive and idealistic, too, and certainly the most enigmatic character in the story, according to Anton Lesser who plays the part.

'There is an air of mystery about Terrell right from the start,' says Anton. 'He doesn't have a lot of screen time initially – just shots of a space-suited figure – but that gets people talking about the character, which is the next best thing. It helps to build up the mystique and sense of anticipation, and when it finally comes out the facts build on the things that viewers have already imagined themselves. Although, ideologically, he has higher aspirations than most of us, he is still a human being with all the same tendencies that we have. He is truly a very complicated and enigmatic man.'

The military dossier on Charles Edward Henry Terrell, British Army officer 520699 – which is actually Jed Mercurio's own serial number from his time in the RAF – is typically brief. Born 13 November 1901. Assigned to the bomb disposal unit of the Royal Engineers at the outbreak of the Second World War. Received a commission in August 1943. Temporarily removed from bomb disposal in August 1944 and 'assigned special duties'. Reported AWOL 26 October 1944 and charged in his absence with desertion. Case never closed ...

Behind these bald statements lies the far stranger truth that in the autumn of 1944, while he was investigating the wreckage of what was at first thought to be a V-1 rocket, Charles Terrell took the first step towards becoming an emissary to the world when it faces a far greater danger than Nazi Germany.

invasion: earth

For Anton Lesser the part of Terrell offered him the unique opportunity to play the same man in two quite different eras.

'Both times that he is on Earth, there is a terrible conflict going on that is foreign to his nature,' Anton explains. 'He just hates what is happening. And nobody will listen to him. He says at one point on his return, "You have come nowhere in all these years – you've learned nothing." '

Anton brings a distinguished film and television presence to the role. On film he has appeared in *One Golden Afternoon*, *Monseigneur Quixote* and *The Missionary*, while on TV he has played a variety of classic and period roles including productions of *Twelfth Night* for Kenneth Branagh, *King Lear* directed by Jonathan Miller, *Anna of the Five Towns* with Martin Friend and Ronnie Wilson's production of *The Mill on the Floss*.

'Terrell has proved to be a quite different part from any I've done in the past,' he says. 'But when I saw Patrick Lau was involved I knew it must be good – he directed *Fragile Heart* which I absolutely loved. So the whole thing came together as something much more intelligent and interesting than I would have thought initially.'

Anton Lesser, director Patrick Lau and Vincent Regan on set in Caterham

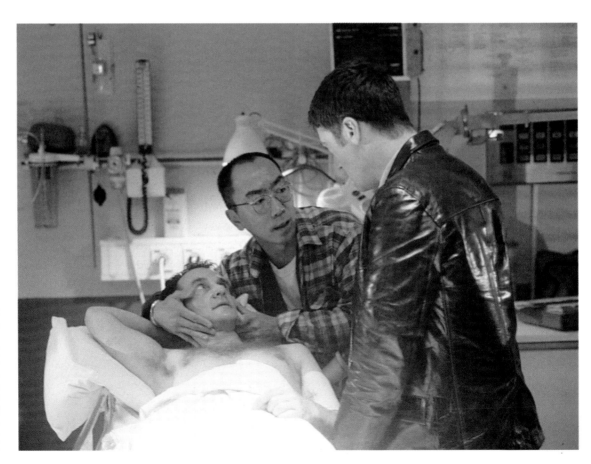

The biggest challenge facing Anton was preparing for the role of a man who has effectively been in space for fifty years.

'You really can't prepare for that,' he admits candidly. 'In a way the best preparation is *not* to prepare – to be as vulnerable as possible. It is not so much about building a character as revealing as much as one dares to. Terrell has been to paradise and back, in a way, and all his sensitivity and ideology has been reaffirmed. It is a struggle to find out who he is.

'He is certainly idealistic and wants to create a different society. He comes back to face the reality of human beings as they are, but he still has this enviable naivety that we might just be able to live together in a more harmonious way. That kind of naivety we could all do with, but the reality of it is that it is human nature to be evil and violent. If only we *did* have his ideals . . .'

For Anton, switching costumes from a wartime officer's uniform to a spacesuit was particularly enjoyable. 'I thought the idea of filming the 1944 episodes in black and white was a brilliant one,' he says. 'It gave the whole story another dimension. You have the dimension from the past which offers more scope to explore the character in his own time. Then he reappears in the present day after what is fifty years but he is hardly a day older. And suddenly he is among men like Drake and trying to find a way to change them from instruments of violence to having a conscience and doing the right thing.'

Invasion: Earth also gave Anton his first experience of special effects. 'I'd never done any of that before and my expectations of how it worked were invariably going to be wrong,' he reflects. 'I thought it would be a case of, for example, being shot in the head and having to undergo a big make-up job. But when it came to it, I was told, "Oh, no, we do all that later with the computer." As an actor that makes you think your job is getting less and less important, really.

'It was also strange reacting to things that were not there. But it is fun and not that difficult. It is just another aspect of the increasingly technical nature of films. It actually makes going back to the theatre very fulfilling because there you are in charge of your entire performance.'

This said, Anton Lesser says he will always remember the series with great affection. 'I think it must be the most enjoyable television job I have ever done. I got on terribly well with the directors and I loved all the toys – playing with all the technology. It was such a professional and friendly set to work on – there was a real buzz about it the whole time.'

TUCKER, Dr Amanda
Civilian Scientific Advisor
[Played by Maggie O'Neill]

Dr Amanda Tucker is the alert and dedicated scientific advisor who is fascinated by extraterrestrial life and messages from outer space. She describes herself as a problem solver with a decided streak in her nature to go against the odds – and authority – when she feels she is on the verge of discovering an unpalatable fact. Amanda is in her early thirties, highly intelligent, and attractive without advertising the fact. She is also a woman who puts up a strong front to get through life, according to Maggie O'Neill who plays the role.

'Amanda is intensely curious about the possibility of alien life,' she says, 'but she is also wary about airing her opinions because she has had her work taken away from her before when it was considered too off-beat by her superiors. She is very careful about that. When her ex-student, Nick Shay, picks up a message from a satellite and they haven't got a clue what it is or where it came from, she is not keen to divulge the fact. However, as she gradually realises that it is probably a message from another planet or life-form with grave consequences for the world, she insists on being at the centre of the resulting action.'

Dr Tucker is also a single parent with a ten-year-old daughter, Emily, and as fiercely protective of the little girl as she is of her career and dreams.

'She is a pretty determined character,' says Maggie. 'She seems to be secure, but I think she is actually deeply insecure. She is determined certainly, but that is driven by her insecurity. And she has her daughter to think of, too. She deliberately got herself pregnant by her tutor at university, but has never lived with a partner. So she has to be pretty independent and make her own way. Amanda puts up this appearance of being very determined and secure and confident, but it is a front in order to get through life.'

Maggie O'Neill herself has shown a single-minded determination in her career since she debuted as an actress on the stage in the Leeds Playhouse production of *Moving Pictures* directed by Annie Castledine. She has since played in a number of classic dramas including *Macbeth* at the Royal Lyceum and *A Month in the Country* at the Cambridge Theatre. Among Maggie's recent films have been *Mona Lisa*, *Gorillas in the Mist* and *When Pigs Fly*. Her television appearances have included parts in the series *Boon*, *Chiller* and *Brother Cadfael*.

Unlike most of the other roles in *Invasion: Earth*, Maggie has not had an on-the-spot expert to turn to in the playing of Dr Tucker. As an experienced actress, though,

invasion: earth

she developed the role from reading and assembling information on the role of a scientific advisor from a variety of sources. The result is a mixture of scientific acumen with feminine resolve.

'I think with Amanda her job is her passion,' Maggie goes on. 'A passion to find out the truth. It is her dream come true when she and Nick discover the signal. From then on she is following her dream no matter where it leads.'

In her quest for the truth, Dr Tucker's path crosses that of Christopher Drake on the same mission, and their uneasy first encounter eventually leads them into each other's arms and a fateful decision in the final episode.

'She is different from other characters I have played because she seems quite held together, while I have tended to play quite emotional characters,' says Maggie. 'But she starts to crack and get more emotional as the story goes on. In fact, she gets abducted and has terrible things done to her – *really* terrible things.'

Maggie shudders at the memory of the scenes she had to shoot as a prisoner in the nDs' world of slime and flesh-like organics. 'It was shocking – really weird,' she says. 'It was a huge set and they had me entangled in this web just shrieking. Because of the use of special effects, I didn't know what it was going to look like at the time – I just had to get right on with it and scream! I remember the first time I did some flying against the blue screen, I thought, "This is a nightmare." But once you've done it a few times, it becomes quite funny. A bit like Peter Pan! In fact, the truth of the matter is that everyone had really good fun during the shoot.'

the INVASION: EARTH

Episode Guide

one

The Last War

A rocket has plunged into war-torn London, 1944. The Army bomb disposal unit who reach the scene think it may be an advanced German V-1 – all of them, that is, except for their leader, Lieutenant Charles Terrell. He suspects the occupants may actually be from another world, perhaps even carrying a message for mankind.

In present day Scotland, Tornado F3 pilot Flight Lieutenant Christopher Drake investigates a breach of airspace over the North Sea to the north-east of Aberdeen. Believing he is about to be attacked, he fires on the unidentified craft, losing his own plane and navigator as a result of the encounter. A metallic escape pod blasts free from the exploding UFO and crashes into a wood in a remote part of Scotland. Here, after a dogged pursuit by Flight Lieutenant Jim Radcliffe and his men, the occupant is finally captured and revealed to be Terrell – virtually unchanged after fifty years.

Meanwhile, a mysterious signal into space transmitted from near the Earth is picked up by computer wizard Nick Shay at a satellite monitoring station. Along

Approaching the crashed escape pod, 1944

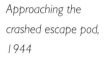
invasion: earth

with his colleague, scientist Dr Amanda Tucker, Nick has been investigating UFOs and the possible existence of intelligent life in the universe. Dr Tucker has had previous work in this area discounted by the 'experts', so she decides to keep the details of the message secret until she and Nick have discovered its meaning. Amanda goes off to Scotland to investigate the possible source of the signal while Nick continues working. He begins to suspect that the signal may have been partially blocked, suggesting not one but *two* forces at work – perhaps even enemies of one another.

At an official RAF enquiry, Flight Lieutenant Drake is charged with disobeying an order not to engage the UFO, and is grounded. Angered by what he sees as injustice, Chris Drake is determined to find out what the other craft really is. By chance he meets Dr Tucker, and apart from being attracted to her, he realises that they are both involved in the same series of events. Major General David Reece from NATO also arrives to investigate the reported UFO and RAF Squadron Leader Helen Knox is assigned as his assistant. She in particular is unwilling to countenance the idea of alien activity. Then the hospitalised Terrell warns the whole group, now joined by Drake and Tucker, that they are in terrible danger. Even as they speak, alien shadows suddenly flood the room where the man from the past is lying . . .

two
The Fourth Dimension

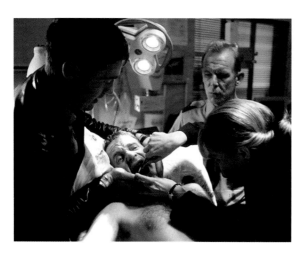

*Tucker removes
Terrell's tooth*

An electronic device is found embedded in one of Charles Terrell's upper molars. Drake suspects it might be a homing device and, with Reece's approval, urges Tucker to remove the tooth for examination. Shortly afterwards, there is another blinding explosion of light and three RAF men, Amanda Tucker and Wing Commander Friday are seized by alien figures and disappear.

When Amanda at last grows aware of her surroundings, she finds herself a prisoner in a weird world that seems to be made entirely of organic tissue. Desperately trying to control her fear, she comes to the conclusion that she must have been seized by creatures whose technology is based on living tissue and she must try to get a message back to Earth. While she is wondering how to do this, the four men are being operated on by unseen hands.

Terrell still refuses to give any information about understand when three of the missing RAF personnel are dramatically returned to Scotland via a dazzling portal of light. The fourth has died, so now only Amanda Tucker is missing. Still captive in the alien world, she realises that her gaolers must exist in a higher dimension of space. She scratches the letters 'nD' on to her bare arm, to signify creatures of n dimensions, as a clue in case she does not survive. But like her companions, she is returned to Earth.

Chris Drake confronts Terrell with the fact that he was the pilot who shot Terrell down. Drake begs him to explain his mission but is met with silence until Terrell divulges his name and serial number. Enquiries by Radcliffe produce an old Army file on Terrell which confirms his role as a Bomb Disposal Officer in World War Two who went AWOL in 1944: case never closed. Drake now suspects that Terrell was probably taken by some friendly aliens – whom he names Echoes – and has returned to Earth to warn mankind of the danger posed by some other utterly ruthless beings. Reece, though, is not prepared to accept this theory.

Meanwhile, a CT scan has revealed a foreign body in Friday's head. Although a scan of Amanda Tucker shows that she has not been interfered with in this way, she is far more worried about the livid wound on her arm and the ominous two letters it bears.

invasion: earth

three
Only the Dead

While Drake and Reece continue to investigate the UFO escape pod, now under tight security at Field HQ, Wing Commander Friday runs amok, shoots a guard and disappears. Radcliffe sets off in pursuit. Amanda, for her part, is convinced that her encounter with the nDs may have made her a danger to Reece's investigation.

Terrell, the Echo and Nurse Louise Reynolds, 1944

119

We flash back to the rubble-strewn streets of London in 1944, where a soldier shoots and kills a figure that dashes from the crashed rocket. Moments later, another staggers out from the pod and Terrell immediately senses that the creature is a wounded alien. His senior officer believes that the aliens are actually freaks from German labour camps being used to test a new secret V-weapon, but Terrell insists that every effort should be made to communicate with the creature. Later, the Echo is taken to a sanatorium where Terrell convinces the shy and delicate being that he is a friend. However, just when he is on the verge of making a breakthrough, Terrell is ordered to return to his unit. However, he has a different destination in mind . . .

Group Captain Susan Preston, an RAF neurosurgeon, arrives at Field HQ to attempt to remove an implant from one of the returned RAF personnel. As soon as she uncovers the implant, it self-destructs and kills the man. Drake suggests that it is the nDs who are inserting these devices to monitor their victims. But *why?*

Nick Shay is summoned to Field HQ and there sets to work trying to activate the escape pod's computer system – which he eventually succeeds in doing for a brief moment. Elsewhere in the complex, Susan Preston and medical officer Flight Lieutenant Tim Stewart are studying the yellow deposits left behind after the alien invasions. They discover to their horror that the cellular structures are identical in every sample, indicating that the nDs are clones of each other. However, what will kill one will kill them all – *if* they can be stopped.

As the group continue to puzzle over the nDs' purpose, another Echo UFO is tracked on radar approaching Earth. Reece orders Drake and Knox to track the craft to its point of impact. They find it in a lake where Drake plunges into the water to rescue the alien pilot. Pulled from the water barely alive, the Echo is rushed to the medical unit at Field HQ where Preston and Stewart manage to resuscitate it.

Terrell speaks a few words with the injured pilot, then dramatically crushes its skull with a single blow of his fist. Desperately saddened but unrepentant of his action, Terrell at last begins to explain his mission on behalf of the Echoes. The Echoes, he has just learnt, have destroyed themselves rather than allow themselves to become the nDs' pawns in their plans to conquer Earth. Terrell explains how he made contact with the aliens fifty years ago and has travelled with them ever since, all the time observing their failing mission against the nDs. His message to mankind is stark and simple: the enemy plan to turn the Earth into a huge 'farm' using human beings as their 'food'.

Unknown to anyone, the stricken Wing Commander Friday has now reached the outskirts of the town of Kirkhaven which will soon become the focus of the invasion . . .

four

The Fall of Man

Susan Preston and her team examine the dead body of the Echo and discover a lump of nD-like tissue on it, corroborating Terrell's story. Reece is still trying to convince his superiors that the space pod is not some advanced weapon developed by a hostile power on Earth, but that the world is under threat of invasion by aliens. Amanda Tucker finds some of the same nD tissue on her wounded arm and allows Tim Stewart to take a sample. She fears that she has been infected and is now somehow being 'processed' for a future task. Drake is anxious to form a plan to draw the nDs into a trap on Earth because they evidently cannot survive long in our atmosphere. Perhaps they would respond if the Echo escape pod were to send out a signal, he suggests?

Amanda Tucker says goodbye to her daughter Emily

Wing Commander Friday is in the last stages of exhaustion. Radcliffe has made contact with Detective Sergeant Rebecca Holland in Kirkhaven in an effort to track him down. Even as they are speaking, Friday uses the last of his energy to slash an artery and fling himself into Kirkhaven Reservoir. The townspeople soon begin to drink the polluted water, and within hours the local GP has an outbreak of 'some kind of bug' on his hands.

Back at Field HQ, Drake and Tucker have set up a communications device taken from the pod which they hope will attract the nDs into a trap: a cage from which there should be no escape. When the aliens initially fail to respond to the signal, Terrell is urged to transmit a message. Almost immediately, the walls of the hangar seem to bend, a blinding light fills the area and an nD emerges to trash the cage and isolation chamber as well as killing a couple of airmen. A hail of gunfire cannot prevent the alien returning to the portal and disappearing. Then, just as the assembled company believe the nD has gone, another portal opens and Terrell is seized. He begs Drake to shoot him as the portal closes . . .

At Kirkhaven, Friday's body has been found in the reservoir. A further investigation of Amanda Tucker confirms her worst fears that the structure of her internal organs is rapidly changing. And despite Drake's tender assurances that Preston and her medical team are working hard to find an antidote, Amanda is left disconsolately believing that she might soon be an alien herself.

Overleaf:
nD wreaks havoc

invasion: earth

five

The Battle More Costly

As Susan Preston and Tim Stewart work on tirelessly, more of the inhabitants of Kirkhaven are going down with the mystery illness. One victim, Jenny Marchant, suddenly disappears outside her home in a searing white light which leaves only an intense scorch mark on the ground. Amanda, growing ever more anxious about her condition rejects all Drake's offers of comfort, unaware that Preston and Stewart have finally discovered a toxin they believe might kill nD cells. Nick Shay has now learned a great deal from the abortive attempt to snare the nD and believes he has found a way of spotting a 'phenomenon' before it opens.

Jenny Marchant is returned to Kirkhaven where the local GP discovers puncture wounds on her jugular vein. The post-mortem on Wing Commander Friday reveals that his whole body had been transformed and turned into a virtual blood-making machine. Reece, fearful that panic may break out in Kirkhaven over the mysterious happenings, decides to post an RAF medical team and put the military on standby.

It is becoming evident that the nDs seem to be after serotonin from the blood of their human victims. While this truth is dawning, Jenny Marchant is once again seized and carried off via a 'phenomenon'. She reappears quickly and is found to be perfectly fit and well. Considering the accumulating evidence, Amanda theorises that the nDs may be filtering off the serotonin because they need it to fuel their biotechnology. And because the aliens cannot survive on Earth themselves, they will probably need human beings to supervise their supplies. Human beings, perhaps, like herself?

Chris Drake goes on trying to convince Amanda of his love for her while continuing his investigations in Kirkhaven. It seems obvious to him that the town has been specially selected as some kind of beachhead for the invasion by the nDs. Radcliffe adds further to the mystery when he discovers that the proportion of men to women in the town has been declining steadily for the past half century.

With Nick Shay's assurance that he has found a way of anticipating the opening of an nD 'phenomenon', Reece prepares to confront the nDs' next intrusion with bullets primed with Preston's toxin. In Kirkhaven, the medical services are being overrun by stricken victims of the infection and some residents have already fled the town. The media, too, have got wind of the events occurring in the little community.

Although the toxin-treated bullets seem to affect several nD attacks, Reece is now in no doubt that Kirkhaven is about to become a battlefield for the future of Earth. And he senses that if the aliens succeed in Scotland, they will probably open a number of other ground stations around the world to complete their conquest. Even as the Major General draws his conclusions, a giant black mass is starting to form overhead.

Drake and Tucker watch and wait for the nDs

six

The Way of All Flesh

A vast 'phenomenon' the size of a hillside has formed over Kirkhaven. Drake and Shay busy themselves by taking soil from near its edge to try to discover what this latest incident in the nD campaign might portend. When Reece orders a military battery to open fire on the 'phenomenon', the shells merely enter it and disappear with no sound of an explosion. The NATO general then cordons off the whole area of Kirkhaven, convinced that its inhabitants have been infected with a disease to enable their bodies to generate the neurochemicals which the nDs need. He also has no intention of underestimating their ability to hit back at any attempts to hold up their plans.

Amanda Tucker is convinced that she is turning into a hybrid life-form who will aid the nDs' plan, and urges the other members of the group to use her as a guinea-pig to find out if there is any way they can defeat the aliens. Nick Shay, unhappy with the military principle of shooting first and asking questions later formulates his own

Battle is underway

plan for making contact with the nDs. Carrying his equipment and radio, he approaches the 'phenomenon' outside Kirkhaven. Moments after transmitting a signal, he is violently seized and disappears.

Tucker suggests a different plan: to fly a probe into the 'phenomenon'. Drake immediately volunteers to pilot the plane himself, but Reece elects to send Helen Knox. She flies in courageously, communicating invaluable data the whole time, until all contact with her aircraft is lost.

Back on the ground, Susan Preston's analysis of the soil sample from beneath the 'phenomenon' establishes that it is draining the land of every living thing. Sadly, she has to admit that her toxin is not the answer to the invasion. Drake, still distraught over losing Helen Knox, wonders grimly if the solution that was employed by the Echoes – total self-destruction – is not the only answer for the Earth, too? Reece reluctantly accepts he may be right and orders a 50-mile exclusion zone to be set up around Kirkhaven. The only weapon he knows capable of devastating the entire area, destroying every living thing and leaving it barren for years to come, is a thermonuclear bomb. But when – and *if* – it is detonated, will it halt the invasion of Earth or merely intensify it?

invasion: earth

CAST LIST

Flt. Lt. Chris Drake	Vincent Regan
Dr Amanda Tucker	Maggie O'Neill
Maj. Gen. David Reece	Fred Ward
Sqn. Ldr. Helen Knox	Phyllis Logan
Lt. Charles Terrell	Anton Lesser
Nick Shay	Paul J Medford
Grp. Capt. Susan Preston	Sara Kestelman
Flt. Lt. Jim Radcliffe	Jo Dow
Flt. Lt. Stewart	Bob Barrett
Air Marshal Bentley	John Shrapnel
Wg. Cdr. Friday	Chris Fairbank
Sgt. Tuffley	Gerard Rooney
Emily Tucker	Laura Harling
Maj. Alexander Freidkin	Jonathan Coy
Gen. Ramsey of Intelligence	Terence Harvey
Echo	Nicola Buckingham
Flt. Lt. Gerry Llewellyn	Stuart McQuarrie
Angela Llewellyn	Valerie Gogan
Sqn. Ldr. Haynes	James Vaughan
S.A.C. Tony Woodward	Graham Bryan
S.A.C. Burton	Luke Garrett
S.A.C. Miles	Tom Freeman
Sgt. Lynch	David Albion
Pte. Grover	Kieron Forsyth
Edward Fleming	Simon Slater
Inspector Boyd	Michael Vaughan
Fighter Controller	Ian Aspinall
Squadron Leader	Miriam Leake
Radio Operator	Jim Pyke
Sarah	Anna Maclay
Grp. Capt. Treves	William Hoyland
Gran	Diana Payan
Sentry at RAF Station	Sean Fall
Civilian Doctor (ep 1)	Selina Griffiths
RAF Doctor (ep 2)	Mark Webb
Nurse Louise Reynolds	Zoe Telford
Motorist	Brian Pettifer
Army Doctor (1944)	Chris Matthews
Det. Sgt. Holland	Nicola Grier
Dr John Vickers	Hugh Ross
Jenny Marchant	Sheila Grier
Receptionist	Barbara Horne

PRODUCTION CREDITS

Writer	Jed Mercurio
Producers	Chrissy Skinns, Jed Mercurio
Director (eps 1-3)	Patrick Lau
Director (eps 4-6)	Richard Laxton
Associate Producer	Alison Barnett
Production Designer	Rod Stratfold
Art Director	Madeline Rogers
Property Buyer	Marshall Aver
Director of Photography	Simon Kossoff BSC
Camera Operator	Julian Barber
Focus Puller	Adam Gillham
Grip	Steve Evans
Editors	Jeremy Strachan, David Barrett
Post-production Supervisor	Alasdair Whitelaw
Composer	Richard G Mitchell
Casting Director	Sarah Bird
Accountant	Guy Barker
Costume Designer	Howard Burden
Wardrobe Supervisor	Gill Shaw
Make-up Design	Tory Wright
Sound Mixer	John Paine
Boom Operator (eps 1-3)	Shaun Mills
Boom Operator (eps 4-6)	John Chandler
1st Assistant Director (eps 1-3)	Simon Hinkly
1st Assistant Director (eps 4-6)	Richard Hewitt
2nd Assistant Director	Steve Robinson
Script Supervisor (eps 1-3)	Maggie Lewty
Script Supervisor (eps 4-6)	Alex Moat
Dubbing Mixer	Steve Haynes
Dubbing Editors	Phil Barnes, Blair Jollands
Telecine Grader	Chris Beeton
Gaffer	Eddy White
Best Boy	Larry Deacon
Location Manager	Peter Tullo
Visual Effects Supervisor	Dennis Lowe
Digital Special Effects	The Moving Picture Company
Special Effects Supervisor	Dominic Touhy
Stunt Co-ordinator	Nick Powell
Opening Titles	Lambie-Nairn
Executive Producer	Andrea Calderwood

With special thanks to the Ministry of Defence, the Royal Air Force and the Queen's Colour Squadron RAF Regiment for their co-operation and assistance.

A BBC Scotland Production in association with The Sci-Fi Channel.

invasion: earth